THE TALKING CURE

A Descriptive Guide to Psychoanalysis

THE TALKING CURE
A Descriptive Guide to Psychoanalysis

Joseph D. Lichtenberg, M.D.

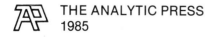
THE ANALYTIC PRESS
1985

Distributed by
LAWRENCE ERLBAUM ASSOCIATES, PUBLISHERS
Hillsdale, New Jersey   London

The Analytic Press

Distributed solely by

Lawrence Erlbaum Associates, Inc., Publishers
365 Broadway
Hillsdale, New Jersey 07642

Library of Congress Cataloging in Publication Data

Lichtenberg, Joseph D.
  The talking cure.

  Bibliography: p.
  1. Psychoanalysis. 2. Psychotherapy. I. Title.
RC506-L524   1985   616.89'17   84-24372
ISBN 0-88163-008-X

Printed in the United States of America
10 9 8 7 6 5 4 3 2 1

Contents

Acknowledgments

My greatest debt is to my analysands, who have both taught me and learned with me to our mutual benefit. The list of teachers and colleagues who imparted their wisdom to me is too long for a prefatory statement. Here I shall single out only Lewis Hill, who taught me that what one does as an analyst is important, but what one is as a person is basic; Heinz Hartmann, whose elegance as a thinker provided a foundation for integrating scientific thought with humanistic sensibilities; and Heinz Kohut, whose revitalization of the concept of empathy has inspired my approach to the analyst's task. A number of colleagues have been unfailingly patient and helpful in responding to my ideas: the late Ping-Nie Pao, Evelyne Schwaber, Ernest Wolf, Warren Poland, Morris Oxman, John Gedo, Melvin Bornstein, Donald Silver, and Jeanette and Nathan Miller. Ann Lichtenberg assessed an early draft of the manuscript to assure its relevance to young professionals. For critical commentary on select chapters, I am indebted to Charlotte Lichtenberg, Rosalie Schonbar, Arthur Malin, and Morton and Estelle Shane. Lawrence Erlbaum, publisher and friend, gave a lift to this project when I needed his faith in order to persevere. Susan Shrader and Paul Stepansky converted the manuscript into a book. But, most importantly, *"The Talking Cure"* bears the stamp of its editor, Susan Heinemann. With her exquisite sensitivity to the reader's need for clear explanations and accessible examples, she greatly aided me in the challenging task of saying complicated things in simple English. To the extent that my penchant for formal psychoanalytic discourse has been softened into conversational prose, it is largely owing to her skillful efforts.

"The Talking Cure" speaks my advocacy of psychoanalysis. On the basis of my more than 30 years of involvement with analysis and psychiatry, I firmly believe that the psychoanalytic experience, when successfully engaged by analyst and analysand, leads to uniquely beneficial changes: the relief of distress through the opening of new possibilities for freedom in one's feelings, one's thinking, and one's capacity for human relationships. As in any other field of organized scientific endeavor, controversies abound with respect to methods, theories, results, and jurisdictions. I mention most of these issues in this work, but do not dwell on them beyond the needs of the lay reader. The picture of analysis that I draw is thus a general one, a kind of nonpolemic consensus to which, I believe, the majority of analysts would subscribe. At the same time, "The Talking Cure" is a highly personal statement, since it derives largely from my own experience as analysand and analyst, student and teacher, listener and guide.

Joseph D. Lichtenberg, M.D.

A Historical Note: "The Talking Cure"

In the nineteenth century the world was turned upside down by two discoveries. The first began in 1831, when the young Charles Darwin set forth on a five-year surveying expedition on the *Beagle*. The surprising outcome of this voyage to the Pacific was the series of brilliant observations that led to the theory of evolution. The second discovery began under more prosaic circumstances. Between 1880 and 1882, Josef Breuer, a prominent Viennese physician, paid daily visits to a bright, vivacious twenty-one-year-old woman who had fallen ill with hysterical symptoms. What was extraordinary about Breuer's venture into Anna O.'s world of hysterical fantasies was his approach: he let her *talk* freely about her sensations, fantasies, and thoughts—and he *listened*. Commenting on the remarkable improvement in her condition that resulted, Anna O. "aptly described this procedure, speaking seriously, as a 'talking cure,' while she referred to it jokingly as 'chimney-sweeping.'"[1] When related later to the young Sigmund Freud, this unprecedented treatment of a neurosis became the observational spark for the discovery of psychoanalysis.

---

[1] J. Breuer and S. Freud, *Studies on Hysteria* (1893–95). In: *The Standard Edition of the Complete Psychological Works of Sigmund Freud*, vol. 2, trans. J. Strachey (London: Hogarth Press, 1955), p. 30.

Introduction

Psychoanalysis aims to relieve emotional distress and improve mental functioning. So do other forms of therapy. Yet psychoanalysis offers a unique experience. How can one describe that experience? In some sense, an experience can never be fully described; it has to be sensed, felt, endured, enjoyed—lived. Still, one may approximate—drawing in the contours, keying the main features, offering the traveler a guide to the land he or she is interested in.

The analogy between psychoanalysis and a journey is in fact a common one. A venture into the unknown of the psyche, a voyage of self-discovery, an archaeological exploration of the residues of the past—all these metaphors have been used to evoke the psychoanalytic experience. There is a sense of anticipation, of the excitement of discovery, but also a tinge of apprehension, the fear of becoming disoriented or lost in traveling into an unfamiliar land. A guide may be helpful—to assure greater success in the exploration and to reassure against losing one's way.

Where does one begin? A large part of this book is designed to guide a person whose knowledge of psychoanalysis is limited. The initial chapters focus on the path to psychoanalysis of someone who seeks help because of emotional pain, a confused sense of purpose, or other problems. How, for instance, does one decide on psychoanalysis as a treatment? Who and what is an analyst? How does one find one? Later chapters explore the psychoanalytic experience itself—a more difficult terrain to penetrate. Volumes have been devoted to a scientific conceptualization of the psychoanalytic experience. Even a preliminary description requires some density, given the complexity of the subject.

Different travelers have different needs. Imagine a group of people interested in visiting a foreign land. Some might say: "I don't know much about this country; tell me about it. What are its major attractions? Its unique features? Its costs?" Others might ask different questions, commenting: "I know most of that already. What I want to know is: what really goes on there? If I visit this land, how can I be sure to get the most out of my trip? What kinds of problems might I encounter? And how do you deal with them?"

This guide is directed toward two groups of readers. The first group is prospective analysands, who want information to determine if the psychoanalytic method is one from which they can expect to benefit. What will analysis do for their problems, for the dissatisfaction and pain they suffer from? How will their thoughts and feelings be responded to? Before embarking on this journey, people may want to feel some certainty that they can fit in with the requirements of analysis. And they may want some assurance that their most private hopes and fears will be dealt with respectfully within a goal of beneficial change.

The second group of readers covers a broad spectrum. College and graduate students, in both the humanities and the sciences, may be interested in a basic description of psychoanalysis, one that gives them a "feel" for the experience, to accompany more conceptual understanding. Psychiatrists, psychologists, social workers, and psychiatric nurses may also want a relatively nontechnical phenomenological description. And, finally, psychoanalytic candidates may desire a presentation of the psychoanalytic experience that covers its essentials in a relatively condensed synopsis.

To guide so diverse a group of readers, I have selected an approach that begins each discussion from the perspective of a person approaching analysis—at first, the curious prospective analysand; later, the analysand involved in the phases of analysis. As often as possible, I illustrate the signposts of my guide with anecdotes and examples drawn from my many years of experience with psychoanalysis as analysand, trainee, teacher, and psychoanalyst. I hope, in this, to make the psychoanalytic experience come "alive." For me, the psychoanalytic voyage is rich in possibility; it is a journey well worth undertaking.

1 Beginning the Search for Help

"People go into analysis because they are in pain," writes Janet Malcolm. "Analysis proposes to relieve mental pain by applying more of the same."[1] What does she mean? Let us begin with the first part of her statement: What is the pain that leads people to seek analysis? It comes in many forms.

Anxiety. For a long time Mrs. Robertson[2] had experienced a sense of dread. It felt as if, out of the blue, something started her heart beating fast. Her chest became tight, her mouth dry, and her swallowing difficult. If it happened during the day, she tried to reason with herself. What was she worried about? Usually she could figure out that it was something to do with her health or the safety of someone in her family. She told herself the doctor said she was all right, or that if anything had hap-

---

[1] Janet Malcolm, "Six Roses or Cirrhose?," *New Yorker* (January 24, 1983), p. 205.

[2] The many examples of analysands given in this book are both actual and fictitious. They are actual in that they derive from the story of an individual or amalgam of individuals with whom I have had contact. All names, however, are fictitious. This and other fabrications are used to disguise the person's identity and protect his or her confidentiality.

pened to the airplane her husband was on she would have heard. In any case, it was easier to hold her anxiety down during the day, when she could distract herself. At night, however, she sometimes woke up terrified, a fragment of a dream half-remembered, half-shrouded in mist. Sleep was through for the night. She tried to read, or write letters, hoping that with morning the feeling of dread would abate. But the nights got worse. And that made the days worse, too. Mrs. Robertson decided she had to find out what her anxiety was really about.

Compulsions. Mr. Daniels sometimes joked that his blood pressure was at the mercy of any fool who didn't have a watch and kept him waiting for an appointment, or any secretary who couldn't set a margin. A man with a great deal of charm, he enjoyed being with other people. But if there was any disruption of the roles and routines he had established for himself and those about him, Mr. Daniels became irritable, sarcastic, and totally intolerant. He did try to control his annoyance, but rarely with much success. Then, after an outburst of temper, he felt regret, suffering from bouts of guilt that were hard to shake. Trying to take himself in hand, he ended up setting even more rigid standards: "I'll have to plan better; I'll give my secretary more careful instructions; I'll call to remind my wife to be on time," etc., etc. At times he told himself that his compulsions were simply the result of his being a serious, conscientious businessman, husband, and father. But he wasn't happy with his anger and his spells of arrogant contempt of others. One day his business partner invited him in for a heart-to-heart talk and suggested that for the good of the company he consider psychoanalysis. Mr. Daniels didn't understand him. What he felt mostly was a compelling urgency to have "order." It didn't cross his mind that his demands, temper, and abrasive manner constituted an illness—one that analysis is designed to treat. What finally drove Mr. Daniels to seek help was the sight of fear in his secretary's face and the tears in his children's eyes. He hadn't fully realized his effect on others before.

Disturbed relationships. Mrs. Green was beginning to feel desparate about her marriage. But she didn't want a divorce.

She had been married twice before and she couldn't bear the thought of a third divorce. The first time, she and her husband were both too young; everyone accepted that breakup. Her second husband was unfaithful; there, too, divorce seemed the right choice. But Alex, her present husband, was a successful, mature man, and they had two children. In the first five years they had been happy. Now, however, they fought all the time, and Alex kept finding more reasons to avoid coming home. Was it something she was doing? She finally confronted Alex, and he had a plethora of complaints, as long as a laundry list. Suddenly she realized that she did too. They went to a marriage counselor, but just continued to fight in front of her. She suggested they both might benefit from individual treatment. Mrs. Green went back and forth in her mind: "Am I a nag as my mother was, or is Alex really inconsiderate? Do I become unduly hysterical over dirt on the children's clothing, as Alex claims, or am I only a conscientious mother? Have I been withholding in my lovemaking, or is it more that I miss the attentiveness Alex showed me before the children?" Deep down she had a lot of respect for Alex—she was certain he really wanted the marriage to work. She knew he didn't want their children to be raised in a divorced home as he and his sister had been. Besides, she had been told for years that she was neurotic and childlike. Painful as it was to look at the problem as hers, Mrs. Green was determined to do so. And with the pain, there was a feeling of hope—the idea that she could change and feel better about herself.

Boredom and general dissatisfaction. Dr. Morton, a respected professor, was embarrassed to admit to himself and to others how empty life seemed to him. He was always being told how fortunate he was. It seemed incomprehensible that despite his inheritance, his academic success, and his well-received publications, he felt blah. Once on the quest of the next distinction, he became energized, convinced that having achieved it he would finally feel fulfilled. Then, when he received it, he felt washed out and depleted, as if it were a setback. Of course with a real setback, Dr. Morton's pride was badly bruised, but that was explicable. It was the dispiritedness he felt with his successes that puzzled him and convinced him that he must be "neurotic." Also, something seemed really wrong with his relations with women. He liked them and they responded to him, but all too soon he felt bored. For a long time he rationalized his boredom as due to the women's shallowness. Then he began to wonder if he were holding back in his feelings, or unable to feel. Certainly he felt devastated if the woman dropped him, but, to be honest, it was more his pride that was hurt than that he missed her. At the same time Dr. Morton was convinced he had more capacity to love and care than he experienced. In a strange way his pain was the lack of pain, and a sense of not tapping in on his deeper feelings or those of others. He was attracted to analysis as a treatment through which he could plumb the depths of his being and, he hoped, make contact with his feeling self.

The stories of Mrs. Robertson, Mr. Daniels, Mrs. Green, and Dr. Morton give a brief glimpse of the kinds of problems that bring people to psychoanalysis. Many more examples might be cited. Dr. Porter, for instance, was so depressed she found it difficult to get out of bed and face another day. Mr. Chambers suffered from premature ejaculation; Ms. Nelson, from frigidity. For all these people, psychoanalysis offered a chance to overcome their difficulties and gain a better understanding of themselves.

But now we come to the second part of Janet Malcolm's statement. How can analysis propose to relieve a person's pain by applying more of the same? On the face of it, that may sound callous. After all, a person in distress craves understanding, sympathy, and relief—not more pain. Actually the word "applying" may be deceptive here. As we shall see, it is the nature of the difficulties, the relative inaccessibility of their underlying causes, that dictates a method in which pain is reexperienced in tolerable amounts. It is never the intent of the psychoanalyst to "apply" pain. The analyst tries to understand the sources of emotional distress and mental dysfunction and, in a caring way, to use that knowledge to benefit analysands. This basic "physicianly" attitude of humanitarian caring is as ancient as human love and compassion. But what exactly makes the treatment psychoanalysis?

DISTINGUISHING PSYCHOANALYSIS

An initial way to approach the question "What is psychoanalysis?" is to inquire into the difference between psychoanalysis and other therapies. Psychoanalysis is the direct outgrowth of Josef Breuer's treatment of Anna O. and Sigmund Freud's extensive studies of the mind. Following Breuer's lead, Freud believed that the common emotional troubles of otherwise well-functioning individuals—the psychoneuroses—were subject to scientific study, explanation, and treatment. By careful attention to his patients' renditions of their thoughts and feelings, Freud concluded that the root of a psychoneurosis was embedded in the individual's responses to life experiences—both traumatic experiences and more ordinary ones. But what was startling was that invariably these responses were related to the patients' childhoods and to their sexual lives; these experiences were influencing them but at the same time unknown to them.

The problem Freud faced was how to get his patients to provide him with information that they had but didn't know they had. From this information, Freud believed he and the patient would arrive at an explanation for the individual's troubles, at an understanding that would bring relief and the possibility of change. Thus, Freud evolved the method called "psychoanalysis." This unique approach to human suffering is not only a technique for relieving pain (a treatment); it is also a way of acquiring data about a type of illness (a research method) and a means of building ideas about the way the mind functions (a psychological theory). Our focus here, however, is on the treatment.

The mainstay of psychoanalysis is the practice of free association. Freud concluded that if people can be induced to say with honesty whatever thoughts come into their minds, the analyst will be able to decipher, from the sequence of associations, a hidden message in which the source of the neurotic symptoms is recorded. Yet for people effectively to direct their attention inward, they must be in a state of relative relaxation, at a distance from the immediate impact of day-to-day concerns. For this reason, psychoanalysis is conducted in a pleasant office setting, with the analysand lying on a couch and the analyst listening attentively, out of the analysand's immediate view.

At this point you may have a lot of questions. Why, for instance, must the person lie on a couch? And why does psychoanalysis require analysands to come four or five times a week over a period of years? Couldn't one come less often and sit in a chair in a conventional conversational mode? It is from precisely this reasoning that the method of helping distressed people called "psychotherapy" has evolved. What is the difference between talking face-to-face with a therapist once or twice a week and freely associating to an analyst four to five times a week?

Psychoanalysis aims to expose the nature of a person's inner struggles. The premise is that once you become aware of what, within yourself, you are afraid of, what you may be fending off or dissociating, you will be freed to resolve conflicts and to restore an integrated sense of self. Thus, analysis deals with much more than symptoms or the immediate source of pain. Very slowly, analysis exposes aspects of personality and character in ways that promote flexibility and choice in patterns that once seemed entrenched and immovable. To accomplish this remarkable change, analysis works with the emotion-laden experience that arises out of the seemingly uncharged task of free association. The very tension that characterizes a person's inner struggles appears in the tension that builds between analyst and analysand in the natural course of an analysis. The very disparities in the self that disturb the person arise during the analysis like a phoenix out of the ashes, and then, with the help of the analyst, become subject to understanding, yielding the potential for change and resolution. For example, during a session, an analysand may suddenly experience anxiety. There doesn't seem to be a "reason" for this anxiety; it is "nameless." The analyst, then, through following the pattern of associations, may be able to interpret connections to definable life experi-

ences—to "name" the anxiety in relation to goals, urges, ambitions, shames, and guilts the analysand has.

How does this experience compare with psychotherapy? In
psychotherapy people also talk about themselves and reveal
their inner secrets. Here, too, the therapist attempts to recognize patterns the person isn't aware of. By clarifying these connections and confronting people with what is revealed about the
sources of their difficulties, the therapist enables them to make
choices that can free them of their symptoms. What, then, is the
distinction from psychoanalysis? Is the difference merely quantitative? Do people receiving psychotherapy get help, but analysands more help? Does coming once or twice a week afford some
opportunity for insight and change to occur, but coming four or
five times a week, a greater opportunity? I believe the answer is
"yes," but I don't believe the quantitative dimension suffices to
characterize the difference. There is a different *quality* to the
experience that takes place in a successful psychoanalysis. The
"more" of analysis is not simply more time or more continuity.
What occurs in analysis is a deeper (and more painful) reexperiencing of past conflicts, combined with determined resistance to this reexperiencing, which makes for a qualitatively
different tension in the analytic relationship itself. All this facilitates the potential for change to occur close to the foundation of
the difficulty. Although many methods bring people relief from
distress, deeply entrenched symptoms and self-defeating personality traits do not change easily. To my mind, psychoanalysis
offers the best hope for their long-term amelioration.

A qualification needs to be added here, for I do not mean to
dismiss psychotherapy. In referring to a therapy usually conducted one or two times a week with the person seated, I had in
mind a particular method of treatment—*psychoanalytically
oriented psychotherapy.* This treatment closely resembles
psychoanalysis, in that it aims to bring about change through
the exploration of unconscious patterns and it uses psychoanalytic theory in explaining the source of the individual's emotional
distress. Thus, many of my statements in subsequent chapters
apply to psychoanalytic psychotherapy as well as to analysis.
Moreover, at times the change-inducing tensions found in

psychoanalysis arise in psychoanalytic psychotherapy as well, thereby blurring some of the lines of distinction. Why, then, might psychoanalysis be recommended for one person and psychoanalytic psychotherapy for another? Or psychoanalytic psychotherapy for the same person at one time and analysis at another? In those instances when the pattern of distress is such that an extensive change in personality seems desired and desirable, psychoanalysis is the preferred treatment. When, however, the need seems more limited, more specific—such as dealing with a particular life situation—psychoanalytic psychotherapy may be the most appropriate form of help. At times neither the person in distress nor the therapist evaluating the person's needs can be certain of the extent of the problems, so psychotherapy may be begun with the possibility of analysis later. Or psychoanalysis might be preferable but impractical—for instance, if an individual won't be staying in the area long enough, or can't manage the number of hours or cost. Psychoanalytic psychotherapy might then be a helpful alternative.

There are, of course, other therapies. Some are as old as civilization, including the power of suggestion as practiced by the shaman or exorcist. Others are much more modern, such as those that systematically induce pain to alter the path of pleasure in some habit such as eating or smoking. Nor is the idea that childhood influences affect adult character specific to Freud or psychoanalysis. It is a theme found frequently in literature. In 1860, for instance, Charles Dickens had Pip, the young hero of *Great Expectations*, say: "My sister's bringing up had made me sensitive. In the little world in which children have their existence whosoever brings them up, there is nothing so finely perceived and so finely felt as injustice. It may be only small injustice that the child can be exposed to, but the child is small, and its world is small."[3] What Freud discovered were specific aspects of childhood centering on sexuality and aggression that

---

[3] Charles Dickens, *Great Expectations* (1860; New York: New American Library, 1963), p. 22.

have a far more profound impact than even creative geniuses like Dickens suspected. Many therapies disagree with this premise or ignore it, trying to work around it through medication, suggestion, or behavioral modification.

Certainly the plethora of therapies to choose from may be bewildering. And obviously I have a bias in choosing psychoanalysis as a focus. But I believe that in gaining a "feel" for what psychoanalysis is, you will be better able to make an informed choice.

ASKING THE FIRST QUESTION: "IS PSYCHOANALYSIS FOR ME?"

We have looked preliminarily at the question of what psychoanalysis is, but there is another, more personal question that each prospective analysand encounters: "Is psychoanalysis for me?" Mrs. Robertson, Mr. Daniels, Mrs. Green, Dr. Morton, each of them wondered: "Can I get the help I want and feel I need through a treatment designed to explore how I think and feel and act?"

In many ways it is fitting that psychoanalysis should begin with this question, for at base it is a method that brings relief and understanding through questioning—or analyzing. At first this question may be just a passing thought, easily dismissed. But with increasing pain, frustration, and doubt, it may become a central consideration, leading to serious self-assessment. Many factors play into the initial push toward psychoanalysis, and sometimes one can only identify these in retrospect. We began with a glimpse of the pain that led Mrs. Robertson, Mr. Daniels, Mrs. Green, and Dr. Morton to the question of beginning psychoanalysis. It may help at this point to describe in a more general way the different forms this question takes.

Symptom Distress as a Motivator

The direct question—"Is psychoanalysis for me?"—often arises at a point where the person is suffering from clear-cut distress. In his original case histories, Freud described a number of "neurotic" symptoms, and any of these may impel a person to undertake analysis. Repeated anxiety attacks, phobias, fits of hysteria, obsessive ruminations, compulsive rituals—these are some of the symptoms commonly associated in people's minds with the need for psychoanalysis.

Other symptoms may take the form of a common physical disorder—the difficulty feels exactly like an ordinary body illness. A man who feels his heart beating fast may fear he is having a heart attack. A woman experiencing breathing difficulty may be afraid that something is wrong with her lungs. When a visit to a physician fails to reveal a medical problem, these people may begin to ask about psychoanalysis. Intestinal upsets, frequent colds or headaches, indeed almost every conceivable physical illness can be simulated or stimulated by emotional factors, with a direct physical cause being absent or minimal. A counter-caution is needed here, however: the emotional distress that leads someone to consider analysis may be part of an illness like asthma or high blood pressure so that it does have a clear physical component. Because many psychoanalysts are trained as physicians, they may be helpful in clarifying this possibility.

The Push of Life Situation Problems

"Neurotic" or "bodily" symptoms are traditionally thought to be the kind of distress that leads a troubled person to consider analysis. Yet in my experience most people, even those who describe specific symptoms, actually seek analysis more for help with general life difficulties than for relief from "symptoms." These life situation problems may take the form of difficulties with work or social or family life. One man was unable to get along with his boss and was repeatedly passed over for promotion despite his great ability. A woman complained of her sporadic achievements; she just couldn't put her potential to use. Indeed, whenever she was on the verge of success, she seemed to sabotage herself. Other people bring up sources of marital distress, including specific sexual symptoms such as frigidity or impotence, and more general difficulties such as coldness or ineffectualness. Another problem may be that a person who wishes to marry finds that, for one reason or another, he or she never makes the right connection.

Despite the diversity of these complaints, there is often a common thread in the motivation to seek analysis. Many prospective analysands, in their self-reflection, begin to realize that there is some pattern to their difficulties, some recurring situation that they get into and know they get into, but cannot seem to avoid. As one person puts it, "I felt like there was a tape in me that kept playing over and over until I was so upset I knew I had to do something to change it."

So far I've focused on problems that are quite noticeable to the person seeking analysis and to others. Many men and women, however, begin to question if analysis is for them when they have only a vague sense of dissatisfaction and boredom, a feeling of flatness about themselves and about life. Dr. Morton was an example. These people speak of a hard-to-define "something missing" in their way of experiencing life. Some may recognize that they tend to "hype" themselves up through one or another thrill—sometimes sexual activity, sometimes gambling or risk-taking "adventure," or, all too frequently now, drugs. Yet none of these thrills is satisfying; there is only a brief, artificial spurt of activity or zest. Why? This question, then, leads to a consideration of psychoanalysis.

When a Latent Motive Becomes a Conscious Question

The ostensible moment when a person confronts the question "Is psychoanalysis for me?" may be when someone else is talking about analysis. Suddenly, the suggestion takes hold; it makes "sense," although the person may not fully understand why.

As a college student in a psychology course, Dr. Rosen had the thought: "Wouldn't it be keen to be in analysis? It sounds like a tremendous mind-trip." That thought was the spur to his beginning analysis. Years later he recalled with amusement how, in convincing himself to start, he had emphasized the intellectual side, ignoring the emotional with all its discomforts. If he were honest now, he had to admit that his keenness also stemmed from the frustrations he was experiencing in his social life and the hope of help.

The question may come up when a physician who has been consulted about physical symptoms indicates that the problem lies in the realm of the mind or the emotions. The person can no longer dismiss this possibility.

Mrs. Janis was listening to her gynecologist tell her for what seemed like the two-thousandth time that her breasts were entirely normal and that there was no reason to repeat the mammogram. As she sat there feeling foolish, Mrs. Janis reflected that under its careful, considerate tone the doctor's voice sounded frustrated and even slightly condescending. She thought: "She's really saying I'm neurotic. Damn it, I know she's right—I'm behaving just like my mother even though I hate to admit it. Bob [her husband] has been suggesting analysis for a year now. It can't be worse than this constant fear of cancer and always running back to the doctor for reassurance."

Or the question may take hold when one is reading a book or watching a movie that makes some reference to psychoanalysis.

Ms. Oxner had just been offered a much-coveted government position. She was sitting comfortably in her apartment, reading D. W. Thomas' *The White Hotel*, when it occurred to her that she did not feel the elation and satisfaction one would expect. In fact, to be honest, nothing in her long list of successes had led to more than a fleeting good feeling. Her mood always turned into a kind of hollow emptiness tinged with depression. That was true even in her childhood. She had always had a feeling of not being complete or whole in some way. Reading about "Frau Anna," Ms. Oxner decided then and there that she ought to look into analysis—the therapy she had had off and on for years had helped temporarily, but it hadn't been enough.

When the question takes hold, it will probably not be the first time it has been considered, however "new" the idea may seem. The decision-making process—considering and acting on the thought "Is psychoanalysis for me?"—usually occurs after there has been an internal working with the question for some time. This is part of what I mean by referring to a "latent motive."

Psychoanalytic theory postulates that in most seemingly spontaneous decision-making, the issue was already in the "preconscious" realm of the mind. That is, it was held in a form of thought-storage; although not in immediate awareness, the idea was there, waiting to be tapped—the way people speak of an idea percolating in their minds. The decision is then "made" when the search beam of consciousness focuses directly on the mental work already going on in the preconscious.

But how, one might ask, does the idea of an analysis start to percolate in the preconscious in the first place? In our culture, at certain levels of society, the fact that people seek psychoanalysis is common knowledge, a familiar subject of general humor, approval or criticism, even in the absence of close personal acquaintance with analysis. Information or misinformation about psychoanalysis is in the air much as the names of Freud, Darwin, and Einstein are commonly mentioned as great men who have affected our modern world, even if details of their exact contributions are vague. Psychological-mindedness about slips of the tongue and dreams has become almost universal. Movies, TV shows, novels, plays, and biographies abound in which psychological motives are attributed to the characters. In fact it may be just that presentation of character that the audience responds to most. So, in reading a book or viewing a movie, one may be simultaneously enjoying an aesthetic experience and stirring up one's own personal problems. Each of us receives a steady flow of stimuli from our personal lives and our recreational activities that build up a storehouse of latent awareness of our emotional reactions—those that bring joy and enhance self-esteem and those that sadden and trouble. If those that sadden and trouble become predominant, the latent awareness may become a spur for an interest in exploring psychoanalysis.

Questioning, Rationalizing, and Procrastinating

When the question "Is psychoanalysis for me?" comes up, it doesn't usually end there. Mrs. Abrams described the route her questioning took in this way: "Oh, I knew I needed analysis— I've said it jokingly for years. I got furious when my husband said it, but, in my head, I really agreed. As far back as college I told my counselor I needed it, but I couldn't do it then. I didn't think my father would pay for it, and there wasn't a psychoanalyst there anyway. Then, when I went to graduate school, I was just too busy. When I started work I told myself if I didn't get married in a year I would do it. But I moved and then I did get married, and at first we didn't have much money and we wanted to buy a house. Now I feel so upset trying to manage my home and my two children plus work part-time that I'm desperate for help, but I don't know if I can find the time. Will all the rearranging I have to do make me feel worse instead of better?"

People like Mrs. Abrams may give themselves or a trusted listener cogent reasons for their belief, extending over years, that they "need" analysis. They may even have made some attempt to seek a consultation. But they always feel their life situation isn't quite right. Indeed, it does seem difficult to work out the arrangements for analysis if one sees oneself as controlled by one's life situations rather than as the one who makes the decisions that control one's destiny.

What were the arrangements that were stumping Mrs. Abrams? As an analysand, she had to be able to commit four or five "hours"[4] per week in the analyst's office, plus the travel time to and fro. She would need to remain in one local for at least several years and to be able to afford a fairly sizable fee. If her arrangements at home (babysitters, etc.) or at work were too chaotic, her frustrations and resentments might interfere with her relaxing enough within the hour to concentrate on the hard task of exploring basic problems.

For Mrs. Abrams, however, all these difficulties could be overcome. The real question she kept turning over and over in her mind was: "Am I really prepared to do this myself? Am I finding excuses because I'm frightened? Do I really want to find out what the problem is? Might it not be better to leave things

---

[4]The analytic "hour" ranges from forty-five minutes with some analysts to fifty minutes with others.

as they are? Or should I face up to what I need to do to make the changes I want?"

Questioning with a "Not Me"

The question "Is psychoanalysis for me?" may also come up in a rather paradoxical form—it may exist as a statement: "Not me! Psychoanalysis is certainly not for me!" Obviously the person is making a judgment, but psychoanalysts would say this person is making a judgment using the negative to tilt the consideration he or she is actually giving to undertaking psychoanalysis. Now, you may well raise an objection: "Here we go again. That's exactly the kind of irritating claim psychoanalysts make that invites disbelief. How can it be that if I tell myself psychoanalysis is *not* for me, I'm actually considering it." The answer isn't really as complicated as it may seem. You can't be thinking about something, positively *or* negatively, without it being a matter under some degree of consideration. Let's take an everyday example. What if you say to yourself, "I will not eat an ice cream sundae"? Aren't you thinking about how nice it would be to eat an ice cream sundae? Sure, you have made a decision about it, a "no" decision. But sometimes, without any further conscious consideration, do you find yourself heading to the store or refrigerator for the very ice cream sundae you've "decided" not to eat?

This brings us to an insight about how the mind works. Frustrating as it may seem, the more one understands some conclusions that analysts have come to, the more one may feel, at least initially, that one is being booby-trapped or caught up in a catch-22 situation. One troubling analytic precept about mental functioning is that, even if one thinks one does *not* want something, the "not" merely says what one is *trying* to do about the wish. "Not" speaks of the undoing of a wish: "I am not angry," "I do not wish you harm," "I am not falling in love," "I am not interested in becoming rich," "I am not politically ambitious"—or "I'm not interested in psychoanalysis." Let me play the devil's advocate. Perhaps you, the reader of this book, would say: "I'm not interested in analysis myself. I just picked this up because I'm curious." Now ask yourself, in full honesty: Is it possible that your curiosity could be motivated by something troubling inside you, something you would rather not, at least at this time, acknowledge to yourself? This question in itself may be disturbing. But it is the kind of question that may lead someone to begin the search for help.

2 Reaching Out—Finding a Qualified Psychoanalyst

"I've thought it over. I've looked at what I know about me—the problems I recognize, the ones I sense but can't define. I'd like to talk to someone, try to understand what's going on. Psychoanalysis seems a possibility. But how do I find out? Whom should I consult? I'm confused about what a psychoanalyst is. Is a psychoanalyst different from a psychiatrist, a psychologist, or a therapist?"

WHAT IS A PSYCHOANALYST?

Many people are confused about what a psychoanalyst is. To begin with, one might define a psychoanalyst as someone whose concern with helping others in emotional distress has led him or her to undertake extensive training in a specific method—one that emphasizes the mastery of emotional problems through understanding. The method and its theoretical basis were discovered by Sigmund Freud. But that is a very general statement. Frequently I am asked: "What is the difference between a psychiatrist, a psychologist, a psychotherapist, and a psychoanalyst?" This uncertainty is not surprising: a psychoanalyst may be a psychiatrist or a psychologist and is in almost all instances also a psychotherapist. To unravel this enigma, the easiest approach is to consider psychoanalysis as a type of advanced training available to individuals who are already specialists in other fields. The three specialty fields from which most psychoanalysts originate are psychiatry, clinical psychology, and psychiatric social work, in that order of frequency. A rough analogy could be made to astronauts—a group of individuals who choose to add to their existing specialties a highly complex, task-focused training. Most have a background as test pilots, but some are engineers and others are medically trained or research scientists.

As noted, the largest number of psychoanalysts have trained as psychiatrists; they are medical doctors who specialized in the care of those suffering from mental disturbances of all diagnostic groupings, using all treatments available. Just as psychiatrists are specialists within the broader field of medicine, clinical psychologists are specialists within the broader field of psychology. Their area of focus is the study of abnormal mental functioning, including the diagnostic evaluation of IQ tests, responses to Rorschach ink blots, and similar measures. Psychiatric social workers, who have studied the individual's relationship to the community or society at large, are specially trained to provide help for people with emotional problems. All three groups—psychiatrists, clinical psychologists, and psychiatric social workers—may receive training within their fields to provide psychotherapy. Put a different way, a well-trained psychotherapist usually holds an advanced degree in either psychiatry (M.D.), clinical psychology (Ph.D.), or psychiatric social work (MSW or DSW).

Now, what about psychoanalytic training? Each group starts with a certain knowledge about treating patients psychotherapeutically. Psychiatrists bring their medical knowledge, including training in a variety of hospital and outpatient techniques and medications. Clinical psychologists possess highly developed skills in diagnosing emotional difficulties and exploring the nature of mental functioning. Psychiatric social workers are familiar with family and group process, as well as pressures and supports from the milieu in which the individual lives. The field of psychoanalysis thus benefits from knowledge brought to it from medicine, psychology, and sociology. And happily the list does not end there. Although not in large numbers, individuals have also received psychoanalytic training whose prior background has been in anthropology, education, law, religion, nursing, and other areas of the biological sciences and the humanities.

Whatever their original discipline, psychoanalysts receive an extensive training—one that requires years. This training is conducted in special institutes, schools, or centers.[1] Here analytic candidates take courses on the theories and method of psychoanalysis. But the mainspring of the training flows from the experience prospective analysts have in their own analyses, increasing their awareness of their own problems and the manner in which the analytic approach opens access to their inner world of thoughts and feelings, needs and urges. Candidates then apply their knowledge and skills to the analytic treatment of others. This is done with carefully selected analysands under the guidance of experienced analytic supervisors.

SCHOOLS OF PSYCHOANALYSIS

Perhaps now you have an idea of what a psychoanalyst is, but you may be perplexed about the several different psychoanalytic theories or schools. There are Jungian, Adlerian, Rankian, Sullivanian, and Kleinian analysts, as well as Freudian analysts. Moreover, as you may have heard, there are heated debates among analysts from the schools of ego psychology, object-relations theory, and self psychology.[1] What does all this mean? And what do you need to know in considering psychoanalysis for yourself?

The history of psychoanalysis has been marked by disagreements over which factors in the individual's development have the most effect on health and distress. In the original group of analysts, Carl Jung, Alfred Adler, and Otto Rank all downplayed the significance Freud gave to sexuality. They each formed separate schools emphasizing other factors; Jung focused on the symbolism of ancestral archetypes; Adler on the

---

[1]See Appendix for a more detailed presentation of various training programs.

significance of urges for power and compensations for weaknesses, and Rank on the trauma of birth and problems of separation. In the U.S. each of these schools has adherents, although the majority of psychoanalysts are Freudian. Yet even within the dominant Freudian group, there are differing positions, despite a shared set of premises.

Because the shared set of premises is central to how the analytic experience evolves, let us begin there. First, there is the concept that all manifestations of mental functioning—all associations, dreams, slips, jokes, symptoms; all feelings and thoughts; all ordinary activities and all creative expressions— are subject to explanation in an orderly scientific manner. This is the principle of *psychic determinism*—that all our mental activity is "lawful," never random or accidental. A second concept is that much mental functioning occurs outside of conscious awareness, that we "allow" certain things to be conscious but "censor" other thoughts. This is the principle of the *dynamic unconscious* and the repression of its contents. Next comes the concept that early events during childhood affect later developments in childhood and that these in turn, consciously or unconsciously, affect how one responds to events in adult life. This is the principle of *epigenesis*, that what comes before exerts an effect on what develops later. A related concept is that the childhood events that have had the most effect on development, whether normal or not, will reappear in disguised forms, affecting all adult human relationships. The psychoanalytic situation is an ideal vehicle for bringing forth these latent childhood configurations, for the feelings toward significant persons from the past tend to be "transferred" onto the analyst. This is the principle of *transference*. Finally, there is the concept that although analysands are naturally eager to rid themselves of distress, they are also reluctant to recognize and abandon distortions from their childhood experiences. This reluctance becomes an omnipresent twin to the revelations made by interpretation of the transference. We call this the principle of *resistance*. Does all this sound enigmatic? As we move more deeply into the analytic experience, this highly condensed set of statements should become clearer. For now they are offered to assure you that adherence to certain broad principles unites most psychoanalysts in the United States, as well as other countries.

Now to the differences. One group of analysts—the so-called ego psychologists—made a prodigious effort to create a balanced, internally consistent and comprehensive theory based on Freud's idea of three psychic structures: the id (our instincts or drives), the ego (an executive and defensive organization), and the superego (our conscience and ideals). In the '50s and '60s this group dominated psychoanalysis in the U.S., although their hold was less in Britain and even less elsewhere. Critics of this remarkably rich and detailed proposal have argued that in one way or another its explanation is too removed from the immediacy of experience. On the one hand, some analysts contend that Freud's original emphasis on the centrality of sexual conflicts has been neglected. Others point to a lack of attention to the influence of aggression, to how destructive forces inherent in our animal heritage affect the earliest stages of infancy. A variety of analysts argue that the actual relations between the child and his or her caregivers should be given more attention. Some would replace the stress on conflict between the mental structures (id, ego, and superego) with a focus on interpersonal relations. Others would retain the emphasis on this internal structural conflict but derive its form and coloring from the infant's relations with the caregivers. They may, for instance, focus on fantasies reflecting the young child's attempts to separate from mother and evolve an individual identity. From yet another perspective, some analysts propose that Freud's hypothetical id, ego, and superego structures be replaced by a concept of states of self-cohesion, determined by the empathic support available from others, past and present.

In considering psychoanalysis, what do you need to know about these schools, theories, and debates? Ideally nothing. Ideally, what matters in each psychoanalysis is the story of the development of the particular analysand. It is a story the analysand tells through his or her associations; one to which the analyst listens, interpreting only in keeping with what the analysand says. Freud insisted that analysts must clear their minds of preconceptions in order to achieve the level of attentiveness that is their unique contribution. But, despite Freud's insistence, the ideal of an analyst constructing helpful interpretations solely from the particular analysand's associations is not subjectively possible (no one's mind works free of prior conceptions), nor would it really be advantageous to the analysand if it were possible. Without preconceptions, analysts would have no way to orient themselves in the maze of associations.

Imagine that you are interested in watching whales or tracking bears. You would want a guide who knew the ways of whales or bears. Similarly, in exploring emotional problems, you would want a knowledgeable guide. An analyst listens carefully to the story of an analysand's struggles and tries to see some direction, some pattern, within that story, based on what he or she has learned about mental functioning—without being limited by these preconceptions. In other words, the analyst uses theory to better discover the analysand's inner world. What the analyst does not do is to use the analysand to confirm some theory in a dogmatic exercise. (Of course, no world is perfect, and there are "bad" analysts just as there are bad doctors, bad teachers, etc.) Regardless of theoretical persuasion, then, psychoanalytic skill and sensitivity lie in a patient, inquisitive listening attitude, an empathic capacity to enter the analysand's state of mind and read and sense his or her distress, without becoming caught up in it. As long as the debate between analytic groups works to increase each group's inquisitive attitude and empathic capacity it works for the analysand's benefit, without the analysand having to know the intricacies of the theories in dispute.

THE OFTEN CIRCUITOUS ROUTE TO FINDING A PSYCHOANALYST

By now you may be impatient. How, practically, do you set about finding a psychoanalyst? Unfortunately, the route to finding a psychoanalyst is often more circuitous than it should be. Many people are accustomed to asking a personal physician for referral to a specialist. Yet all too often family doctors have only limited knowledge of analysis and analysts. Of course, a well-informed physician is likely to be an excellent referral source, and may even provide expert medical reassurance and care during the analytic experience, especially if it stirs up anxiety about bodily symptoms. But what if a knowledgeable physician is not available? Many people turn to friends and acquaintances: "Oh, I remember talking to Mark's sister at the reception. She's a psychiatric social worker and she mentioned being in analysis. I could call her." Or: "My cousin in Chicago is married to a psychiatrist. I could call him and see if he knows a psychoanalyst here."

At this point you may have another question. Beginning psychoanalysis is usually a somewhat frightening venture, no matter how determined you are to find the source of difficulties. The question at the cutting edge is: How do you find an analyst whom you can depend on to understand and help you? You may have the thought: "I know there are good lawyers and not so good lawyers, good engineers and not so good engineers, good nurses and not so good nurses. There must be good psychoanalysts and not so good psychoanalysts or at least psychoanalysts who would be good for me and some who would not be good for me. So how do I find one who is not only good in his or her profession but good for me too?"

APPRAISING THE ANALYST'S TRAINING

As a first step, you may want to find out about an analyst's training. Unfortunately, in some states there is no law to prevent someone from using the title "psychoanalyst," whether or not the person has received psychoanalytic training. Surgeons who have completed their training and passed their specialty requirements are listed as certified by the American College of Surgery; psychiatrists are certified by the American Psychiatric Association; and so on. Isn't there a book in which you can find out if a psychoanalyst is a certified practitioner? At least that would tell you if an analyst had completed training in accordance with standards set by an established organization.

One book offering such a listing is the Roster of the American Psychoanalytic Association. The American Psychoanalytic Association (the organization to which I belong) is a federation of individual psychoanalytic societies (see Appendix). These societies are located in the major population centers, such as New York, Chicago, and Los Angeles. Each has or is affiliated with an institute or educational training center. As I stated before, analysts in training attend classes and treat patients using the psychoanalytic method under the supervision of experienced teachers. When a candidate has successfully completed the class work (usually three to five years) and has demonstrated competence in treating different types of emotional problems (usually five to eight years, rarely less, often longer), he or she graduates from the local institute. The candidate then applies for certification by and subsequent membership in the national organization. Standards for the teaching and training procedures followed in the local institutes are set by committees of the national organization. Committee members make regular visits to each institute to evaluate the training programs.

Thus, one way you can be assured that the person whose name you have been given by your physician or Mark's sister has received a formal training is to look him or her up in the membership roster of the American Psychoanalytic Association or in the roster of one of the affiliate societies. But if you don't find the name there, that doesn't mean the person hasn't received competent training. You might want to consult the lists of other well established training programs (see the descriptions in the Appendix).

But what about finding the psychoanalyst who is good for *you?* You are considering starting a treatment that involves intimate personal revelations and interchanges. A name on a list is impersonal, to say the least. Moreover, regrettably, all the standardizing and testing in the world does not prevent inadequate individuals from occasionally slipping through. In the end you will have to rely on your own judgment. Still, there are questions you can ask to help you make that judgment.

3 Reaching Out—Seeking the Qualified Analyst You Prefer

Let's rephase our question: How do you find the psychoanalyst you want? One way of looking at this question is to weigh the different variables in terms of their importance to you. Certainly you want someone competent, and we have already touched on the question of training. Beyond this, however, you may have other questions.

SHOULD YOU LOOK FOR THE "BEST"?

Mr. Carter, a top executive in a multinational firm, knew exactly what he wanted his psychoanalyst to be. He wanted him to be the best. Thus, he made unusually extensive inquiries about the reputations of the analysts in his area. One analyst in particular—Dr. Smith—was mentioned favorably numerous times; he was considered the "dean" of analytic practitioners and described as the analyst's analyst. Satisfied that now he had the best, Mr. Carter arranged for an appointment, which required a considerable wait. He protested and attempted to use various means of persuasion to effect a special early meeting. Yet when his tactics failed, he settled down to wait, reassured that indeed this analyst was in demand. Finally, the day arrived; Mr. Carter went to the analyst's office. As the door to the waiting room opened and the analyst entered, the executive pulled himself to his full six feet two inches in preparation for shaking hands. Dr.

Smith, a short, unprepossessing-looking man, noticed the consternation on the face of the prospective patient as they greeted one another. With a whimsical smile, the analyst is reported to have said, "Well, come in anyway." Warmed by Dr. Smith's gentle, ironic humor and intuitive understanding of his startle, Mr. Carter did go in. Thus began what proved to be a successful analytic relationship.

DOES GENDER MATTER?

Some people considering analysis may have no strong preference if the analyst is a man or woman. For others, however, this may be an important variable. One woman, for instance, may feel the dominant figure in her life, the one from whom she has derived her greatest sense of security and strength, is a woman. She may thus prefer a female analyst. Another woman may view the dominant male in her life as threatening or untrustworthy and painfully disappointing; she, too, may prefer a female analyst. One man may feel he cannot possibly reveal his innermost thoughts, especially his violent rages, to a woman and so may consider only a male analyst. Another man may believe a woman would be more sympathetic warm, and comforting, although he might go to a man who struck him as friendly.

These concerns about gender both indicate the effects of past relations and foreshadow what is to come. As indicators of the past, they will need to be worked with over time and understood—that is, "analyzed." As foreshadowings of the future, they require respectful attention in the period of preparation for analysis. There is so much of an intuitive "feel" in at least the initial relatedness of two people that an analyst and future analysand should begin, if not with a sustaining positive feeling, at least without an aversion on the part of either.

WHAT ABOUT AGE?

The age of the analyst may also be a criterion. The average age of psychoanalysts when they finish training is forty, with thirty-five probably the younger limit. On the upper end, many analysts continue to practice into their seventies and occasionally into their eighties. One person may be comfortable with a younger analyst, believing that someone closer in age will understand his or her particular problems better. Another person of the same age, indeed one with very similar problems, may feel more comfortable with an older analyst. This person may believe that an older analyst's broader experience will prove an asset.

Of course, these preliminary beliefs may prove to be illusions. One young woman in her early thirties was pleased to begin her analysis with an older analyst, feeling she could rely on his steadiness and experience. She discovered, however, that try as hard as she might she could never bring herself to be fully open with him about her past sexual experiences and current sexual thoughts and feelings. She rationalized that his age made him seem too austere—too likely to be shocked, offended, even outraged at her "shameful" sexuality. After moving to another city she carefully selected a "not-so-old" psychoanalyst, only to discover that before long she began to experience the same reluctance. Now it seemed to have less to do with the analyst being shocked because of his "advanced" age, but more because, being "younger," he was clearly the figure toward whom many of her feelings became directed. It is worth noting that this woman's recognition of the way she had reacted to the earlier experience helped her to resolve the new impasse with her second analyst.

WILL RACE, ETHNIC BACKGROUND, OR RELIGION HAVE AN EFFECT?

Again, the analyst's race, ethnic background, and religion may be important criteria from some prospective analysands and not for others. Going to a black analyst may seem out of the question for some white analysands, and vice versa. For others, it may be a matter of initial strangeness, but have no great effect on the analysis thereafter. A prospective analysand of Asian origin may wish to find an analyst from the same country, not only for a feeling of camaraderie in a strange land, but also for his or her cultural orientation to be appreciated and to be able to communicate bilingually.

A Japanese-born man, for instance, asked if he might see an analyst of Japanese origin or one familiar with Japanese culture. He had been in psychotherapy with a kindly woman, but they had come to an impasse over his problems with dating. She had treated it as defensiveness and sexual inhibition on his part when he did not respond to the obvious overtures of a forthright American woman. He disagreed, knowing that he was responsive when the cues followed the pattern of more subtle, shy flirtation and the particular gestures of his culture. He hoped to work with someone who understood this so he could get on to the problems in relationships he knew he did have.

The analyst's ethnic background and religion may also elicit strong positive or negative reactions. A first-generation American–Irish Catholic patient requested an Irish Catholic analyst or a Jewish analyst, in that order. She felt an "establishment WASP" would understand her least. A Jewish professional man, whose family had barely escaped Nazi persecution, insisted that his analyst be Jewish. When this was arranged and he entered analysis, however, the religious issue quickly turned from a feeling of compatibility to one of increasing distance and suspicion. Whereas he was an Orthodox Jew, he concluded his analyst was Reformed. Whereas he was of recent Eastern European origin, he concluded his analyst was of German Jewish extraction, with several generations in America. For this man, religion and ethnicity stood in a symbolic, condensed form for many different conflicts. His identity as a Jew was both a source of great pride and security and a source of potential embarrassment and great fearfulness. What happened was that the analyst's presumed religious affiliation provided the "battleground," against which many of this man's conflicts both about religious identity and about self-esteem in general were brought out and interpreted.

This example illustrates how complex the issue of preferences often proves to be, as unconscious meanings commonly underlie the consciously known request. In this instance, the wish for a Jewish analyst had been acceded to, and a sense of successful

working together had consolidated before the "battle" developed. Thus, there was a background of a cooperative alliance
to sustain the analysis when the fearfulness came to occupy the
foreground.

HOW IMPORTANT IS THE ANALYST'S PERSONALITY?

For some people, the question of which psychoanalyst to choose
centers on the analyst's personality traits and attitudes. One
expects an analyst to be capable of essential warmth and caring,
to be interested, understanding, and actively concerned. But
what does one take as signs of this? To one person, a welcoming,
cheery approach may affirm warmth and interest. To another,
however, this approach may evoke fears of shallowness, hypoc-
risy, or seductiveness on the analyst's part. Over time I have
learned that although I believe I approach each person seen in a
consultative interview in essentially the same way, one may see
me as pleasant, professional, and caring while another initially
sees me as cold, computerlike, and formal.

Moreover, either the "warmth" or "coldness" may attract or
repel. One young woman told me she decided to begin treatment
with me because my professional manner made her feel she
would not be able to manipulate me in the way she had
manipulated her father and other men. Another told me she
chose a colleague who struck her as more informal and talkative
than I.

I believe the feel-of-the-person reaction is important to consider, although it must also be regarded within a larger perspective. In the larger perspective are the analyst's ability to adopt a
consistently effective listening stance, to sort out what is heard,
and to interpret tactfully and clearly. This of course can at best
be only guessed at by prospective analysands from their initial
reactions.

Other traits of the analyst may evoke unexpected responses
in a particular individual. One man I referred to a colleague
came back for another referral. It turned out that the appearance of my colleague's personal attire and his office conveyed a
sense of a highly cultivated neatness and precision—a decorator

look. This man was seeking treatment after a painful marriage breakup. He and his wife had had a continuous argument centering on his "casualness" and her "stylishness," like Oscar and Felix in the *Odd Couple*. He was not really looking for a sloppy analyst—only one who did not seem shockingly like his estranged wife. He accepted the next referral.

None of this is to say that prospective analysands are excessively demanding about the analysts' particular characteristics. That has not been my experience. My examples of intense reactions are meant simply to illustrate issues of preference that I believe to be general. All too often a person considering analysis does not actively contemplate his or her preferences beforehand. As a result, the prospective analysand, the referring source, and the consulting psychoanalyst can't evaluate this factor. Generally, I try to find out what a person's preferences are. Even if it isn't possible to meet these preferences, most people will make adjustments with good grace, especially if they feel their wishes have been recognized and given reasonable consideration. If, however, a person feels that a matter of personal importance has been waved aside in an imperious, condescending, or patronizing fashion during the consultation, the subsequent treatment may be burdened by resentment.

WHAT OTHER ISSUES AFFECT PREFERENCE?

Sometimes the preferences of a person considering analysis may revolve around an emotionally charged topical issue. One example comes from a number of years ago. A man in his thirties sought analysis because his marriage was disintegrating. An early, vociferous opponent of the Vietnam War, he felt he could not possibly work with an analyst whose personal convictions were at marked variance to his. As it was, he had to confront continued resistance to his views from family members, friends, and professional associates, with implied or direct accusations that his political and moral position was neurotic. Maybe some of it was, but he did not want his analyst to put him in the same defensive position others did. Although this man recognized the need to try to understand the meaning of his strongly held opinion, he feared that an analyst whose politics were strongly opposed could divert him from working on the problem he was primarily concerned about—the breakup of his marriage.

A more recent emotional issue is the women's liberation movement. On the basis of intense commitment to the social changes involved, some women considering analysis have demanded a woman analyst who shares their position. Others want to know if their prospective male analyst is in agreement. Still others do not raise the issue of women's progress directly, but specifically ask not to be referred to an analyst who believes in "penis envy."

Any preference, especially an emotionally charged one, requires a good deal of thought on your part. Obviously, in entering analysis, you want to feel as comfortable as possible, that you can be true to yourself. At the same time there needs to be an understanding that analysts are trained to recognize and limit interference from their personal value commitments in order to more fully enter empathically into the analysand's attitudinal state. You can expect your analyst to respect your wishes as having subjective meaning and your serious convictions as indicating your search for moral and ethical ideals. But it is also important to recognize that strongly held wishes and convictions may be derived from sources outside conscious awareness. These unconscious sources may even be at considerable variance from the reasons you would consciously give yourself.

The presence of known and unknown sources for wishes, aims, and values follows the psychoanalytic principle of "multiple determination." It states that all our persistent desires, actions, and convictions gain their strength from multiple motivational sources coming together. Under optimal conditions, unity of action and conviction comes about when wishes, as well as imperative bodily needs (such as hunger or the urge for sexual release), combine with purposes, plans, and functional capacities under the guidance of ethics, morals, and ideals. But such an ideal confluence rarely happens; it cannot be assumed, without reasonable reservation, to be the *sole* basis for a strongly held preference. A person's strongly felt request may indicate both an accurate intuitive sensing of a helpful match and the play of forces possibly at variance to the conscious positive goal.

What is the analyst's role here? Analysts do not take a doctrinaire view that a person's preference is either "normal" or "neurotic." And it is this nondoctrinaire, nondogmatic view that you can expect on such issues as the Vietnam War, women's lib, and penis envy. Analysts try to use their knowledge of social norms and human development to orient themselves to the meaning of an analysand's associations. To dogmatically superimpose one's own preconceptions on the analysand's communications is opposed to the investigative approach of psychoanalysis.

4 The Consultation

"At last I've found a possible analyst. I've telephoned and set up an appointment for a consultation. What can I expect from the interview? What will happen? What can I accomplish?"

The consultative interview provides an opportunity for two people, a prospective analysand and a psychoanalyst, to get together to pool their information and arrive at a mutually agreed-upon conclusion of use to the person seeking help. Yet, in anticipation, the prospect of a consultation seldom feels reassuring to the person contemplating treatment. Many people feel a cross between anxiety at facing an "examination" (one might be found unacceptable or "sicker" than expected) and apprehension at embarking into the unknown. Small wonder then that, for many, in coming to the first consultative interview, a funny thing happens on the way to the office. "Oh, I lost my way and I must have taken a wrong turn." "I'm sorry I'm late. I thought I had enough time, but I discovered I didn't have enough gas in the car so I had to stop." "When I was sitting in your waiting room I suddenly had the thought, this isn't the right day. Then you came out. I was relieved." Analysts are familiar with the mixture of apprehension and doubt people bring to the consulting room. Usually, as a first step, they will attempt to make the experience more comfortable. In a sense that's what I hope to do here, by drawing a picture of what you might expect.

THE CONSULTING ROOM

Knowing about the physical setup often helps to reduce a feeling of initial strangeness, so let's look first at the most common office arrangements. The office may be located in the analyst's home, in a separate apartment building, or in a university or hospital building. Usually, there is an entry door with the analyst's name on it. Then there may be an entry hall with a place for coats and off of it a waiting room. In that case, you enter and leave by the same hall so you can leave your coat there during the interview. Alternatively, you may enter directly into a waiting room and then go into the consulting room and leave by a separate exit. Sometimes a group of analysts share a suite and have a common waiting room. There, or in a university or hospital setting, there is often a receptionist. Otherwise there generally isn't. Most commonly there is a lavatory available off the waiting room.

The consulting room is generally set up as something like a comfortable den, with bookcases and pictures on the walls. Unlike the offices of other doctors or professionals, here diplomas and certificates are rarely displayed; the look tends to be less "formal," without medical austerity or antisepsis. During the interview, the person sits in a comfortable chair set in a conversational arrangement with the chair the analyst uses. A point of emotional focus may be "the couch," but this is not used until analysis is decided on.

Every consulting room is different—although the overall effect is usually both restful and professional. After all, the consulting room is a place where the particular analyst spends many hours. In it, for his or her pleasure, the analyst may keep pictures and objects to look at and journals to read. On the other hand, it is designed to be shared with patients, as a place conducive for contemplative investigation. It is thus both a distinctive but unintrusive representation of the analyst's personality and a setting in which the analysand's personality may expand relatively freely. In the beginning it may offer reassurance: "If you are uncomfortable, just sit in this comfortable chair and relax so you can deal with this person sitting nearby but not pressingly close." Or it may extend an invitation: "If you aren't too uncomfortable, look around. This is a place in which you may choose to spend a lot of time. From it you can discern something of the taste of the person you will be working with intimately." Analysts are of course individual people, with their own individual characteristics and tastes, even though they will not try to impose their ideas on you. Like the room, the analyst conveys a presence, but also a neutrality that may put you at ease. In this regard, you probably won't see personal pictures or much that reveals the analyst's private life.

If you decide to begin analysis, you will find that this room is also a place in which items, once introduced, rarely change. As one analysand, well along in her analysis, commented: "This room is, for me, like a space capsule. I enter it and I feel closed in, protected. There is movement relative to the outside world, but inside here it's like a time warp. I stay in the present at the same time that I go backward into the past and project myself forward into the future. Then the hour ends and I stand up. And here I am in this same old room where the plant grows and the books go up and down on the shelves, but nothing ever changes and yet everything changes too. I'm going to miss it when I'm finished."

One final word about the physical setup before we go on to the interview. As may already be clear, each detail is designed to facilitate a person's entry into the analytic process. The setting is one conducive to introspection. And it aims to create a sense of professionally controlled intimacy with another human being—the analyst—while offering privacy from all others. In my own arrangements, for instance, I prefer a private waiting room where the analysands can come some moments before the hour, sit alone, and collect themselves. They may glance through a magazine or relax and think. In this way they can make the transition from the exigencies of everyday life, from the pull of the immediate and the practical, to become reflective and communicating that reflectiveness.

I also try to set it up so the analysand seated in the waiting room does not encounter the person leaving the consulting room. To some degree this is to protect the anonymity of each, but of course this can be done only within limits. Usually, over a period of time, two people coming and leaving the same place on a fixed schedule will run into each other. Primarily, I aim to provide both the analysand coming in and the one leaving the psychological time and space to compose themselves. The person leaving can benefit, I believe, from a bit of space to move in before having to suppress the emotions with which he or she ends the analytic session. As one analysand put it, he did not like to have to put his "face" back on when leaving the consulting room. In the hall, as he put his coat on, he would take a first step—get rid of tears or whatever. Then he liked to keep the mood and reflect until he left the building and got into his car.

BEGINNING THE INTERVIEW

Now let us return to the waiting room. Pretend you are anticipating your first consultation. Perhaps you hear the doors opening and closing; the person before you is leaving. Then the waiting room door opens; the analyst enters to greet you.

Here each analyst is different, and for me each situation is different. Invariably I say the person's name to establish his or her identity and then introduce myself. Whether I shake hands or not depends on the leads, the "feel," I get. In any case, I invite the person to enter the consulting room and indicate which chair to sit in. At some point the basic information of correctly spelled name, address, phone number, and age is written down. But if this comes at the beginning, the pad is soon put aside and the business of the interview is gotten to. Some people are ready to begin spontaneously, and I let them go ahead. If, however, someone is demonstrably uncomfortable, I ask about his or her feelings and try to put the person at ease. Generally I simply begin the interview by asking the person to tell me about his or her reasons for consulting me. The purpose at this point is to encourage a relatively spontaneous, one-sided informational flow.

Different people pick up on different emphases in my question about the reasons for consulting me. Some begin to tell me about their problems. They may describe their symptoms, relate the details of a situation that troubles them, or convey the pressure being placed on them by family, friends, or an employer to seek help. Others, however, pick up on the *me* side of the question, indicating how they got my name and came to call me. Both types of information are useful.

What is it, then, that the analyst needs to learn? Basically, the analyst is trying to acquire a broad outline of information about the person that will help in making a recommendation. Often this takes more than one interview session. The analyst wants to find out about the person's current problems and the timing and circumstances of their onset—the first part of my question. But the analyst also wants to know how the person makes decisions—the second part of my question. As the individual talks, he or she usually reveals facts and feelings about significant life events, as well as about family members and others who have been important. The person's education, main interests, physical health, religious orientation, and future plans and hopes, all these, it is hoped, come to be sketched in, at least in a general summary form.

WHAT KINDS OF QUESTIONS DOES THE ANALYST ASK?

How does the analyst set about acquiring all this information? Different people have different styles. In describing their problems, some move easily into ever-broadening areas of their lives, making pertinent connections to the past. Others have a more abbreviated style, so the analyst may use a question to elicit more information.

Many of the questions the analyst asks will be only minimally directive. For example, if it has not been described spontaneously, I might ask: "Can you tell me something about your background?" In response, the person may relate specific facts: "I was born in Media, Pennsylvania. I went to parochial school there and then on to Fordham in New York." Another may offer a glimpse of family life: "My parents were first-generation immigrants from Poland. My father died when I was nine, and my mother held the family together. She was a pillar of strength." Yet another may reveal a personal reaction: "There were eight of us kids and since I was the oldest boy a lot was expected of me. If it hadn't been for the Monseigneur in our town, I wouldn't have been able to stay in school. But he got me scholarships. I always felt I had to work day and night in appreciation." Each response provides information on many levels. The first answer, for instance, suggests something in what it doesn't say; the second and third, in the focus chosen.

The information sought is only partially the "facts." For the analyst, the point of the consultation is not to fill out a conventional medical-psychiatric history form, but to learn about the person as a person. This kind of information can't be gained through an organized, formal sequence of questions. Instead, the analyst invites the more or less spontaneous flow of the individual's thoughts and feelings, formulating his or her questions in accordance with that flow. Based on the way the person responds to a question, as well as on the information he or she selects to tell, the analyst tries to discern patterns that give meaning to what is said.

Here it might be helpful to enter into the analyst's state of mind. As the analyst listens, he or she may muse over a number of questions. Does the pattern of distress in general and, more important, the particular form it takes in this person lend itself to psychoanalytic resolution? And is psychoanalysis possible on a practical level? Will the sacrifices of time, money, and emotional investment required for psychoanalysis be too much, leading to resentment? Or do this person's everyday resources and motivation for change augur well for such an undertaking? What about my working with this person? Practically, could we set up a suitable schedule? And does an emotional "fit" seem to be present, or is there something in the person's preferences that might go against this? If a suitable practical or personality mix does not seem present, the analyst might think about a referral to a colleague. Who would be most likely to meet this person's needs? If, on the other hand, psychoanalysis itself does not seem possible, for whatever reasons, the analyst might contemplate an alternative mode of treatment. As mentioned earlier, psychoanalytic psychotherapy is one possibility.

HOW DOES THE ANALYST ARRIVE AT A DIAGNOSTIC IMPRESSION?

The word "diagnosis," with all its medical connotations of disease, may seem alarming at first. Let me clarify what I mean. First of all, I am speaking of a diagnostic *impression*—a kind of working hypothesis about what the trouble is. Only in the course of an analysis, as the analyst learns more and more about the analysand's problems, wishes, dreams, and fantasies, does a clearer picture emerge. The idea is not to slot the person into some category, as having this or that "illness." The aim is always an understanding of the individual. What a diagnostic assessment does, however, is to help the analyst to relate a person's particular situation to other, similar situations. It can be reassuring to know that other people have similar difficulties, and one can learn from their experiences. Keeping my cautions about the dangers of preconceptions in mind, one could say that a diagnostic assessment enables the analyst to bring knowledge about human functioning in general to bear on the particular individual's dilemma.

To form a working diagnostic impression, the analyst usually need do nothing more than listen, letting the pieces fall into place, asking a focused question here and there to corroborate the assessment. For the most part the analyst arrives at an initial assessment relatively quickly—within one to three consultative interviews. An analyst who is unsure about his or her diagnostic impressions may extend the consultation period or, in some instances, suggest psychological tests or a consultation with a colleague.

But how does this diagnostic impression relate to the person seeking help? During the consultation, at a point when the major information has been gathered and I feel that my impressions have been confirmed, I offer the person a diagnostic appraisal. By choice I do not use the technical terms of a diagnostic manual. In my opinion, they are subject to confusion and misinterpretation. Rather, I offer a diagnostic "summary": "From what you've told me, I gather that the anxiety attacks and your fear of cancer began after the birth of your second child. Before that you mentioned you were inclined to be fearful, especially when you went away to college and when you went on dates, but you could control that anxiety. You began to feel harassed with the care of your second baby; you described feeling trapped and having bitter fights with your husband, who was perplexed at the change in your mood. You made the suggestion, and I think it's a good one, that your reaction is in some way connected to your mother's illness after the birth of your younger brother and your feeling then that you had to be terribly grown-up and supportive of her. You described your father as the great hero of your life then, but he was often inaccessible, especially after your mother became ill." I then let the person react to what I have said. After some further discussion, the conversation turns back to my offering a recommendation. I might summarize: "In all, what you say about your present problems and your past experiences indicates to me that psychoanalysis would be the best treatment for the difficulties you have."

HOW DOES THE ANALYST ARRIVE AT A RECOMMENDATION?

Earlier I mentioned some of the questions that go through an analyst's mind in deciding on a recommendation. Let's take a closer look at the factors the analyst must consider. Although the pattern of the person's difficulties may suggest that psychoanalysis is appropriate, other variables must be weighed. The person's life situation may seem too chaotic—a mother may be the only one in the home to tend her physically ill child or a man may be in a frantic state, his partner having died, requiring him to devote heroic efforts to salvaging the business. In these instances the individual would benefit from a period of psychotherapy, receiving help to stabilize the current situation. This might then serve as preparation for analysis at a later time.

Another factor weighing against analysis would be if the person seems unlikely to remain in the area for an adequate time. Or the person's time commitments and financial limitations may preclude the undertaking on simply practical grounds. On a different level, if it becomes apparent that the person is poorly motivated, feels pushed into the consultation by someone else, or is seeking a magical cure, analysis will not work. Yet another factor the analyst tries to assess is the special kind of skill that enables an analysand to work well within the analytic method. This difficult-to-define skill is often called "psychological-mindedness." Basically, it is the ability to associate freely and to make emotionally meaningful psychological connections. It has been suggested that this capacity is less likely to be found in "hard" science practitioners, engineers, and computer experts than in "soft" scientists, mental health professionals, and artists. In my experience, such a dichotomy is not accurate. The kind of wit and sense of humor that it takes to laugh at jokes, the willing suspension of disbelief that allows a person to enjoy the theater, these are indicators of the psychological-mindedness. Self-reflectiveness, imaginativeness, and awareness of one's daytime fantasies and night dreams are further indicators. And curiosity, both serious and playful, is a valuable component of the "mind-set" that makes for an affinity to the psychoanalytic method.

How does one appraise a person's skill in thinking psychologically? Sometimes I ask a question which may lead in this direction: "Do you believe that being an only child has played a part in the way you respond to situations?" Or: "Looking back on it, what do you think may have been the source of the tension between your mother and father before their divorce?" Or: "How do you account for the change between high school, where you were an indifferent student, and college, where you blossomed?" In using questions like these, I am not interested so much in the answer itself, but in the approach the person takes in formulating his or her response. Will this individual's way of thinking and feeling fit in with the requirements of an extensive introspective inquiry?

HOW DOES ONE ASSESS THE PERSONALITY FIT?

Assessing the match between the personalities of the anlyst and the prospective analysand presents another kind of challenge. Ther are two viewpoints we need to consider—the analyst's and the prospective analysand's.

The Analyst's Assessment

A revered teacher of mine advised: "Never take on as an analytic patient a person with whom you feel inclined to fall in love or to hate at first sight." He was identifying emotional responses to an analysand that interfere with an analyst's ability to focus his or her attention properly. I would add that, as an analyst, one should never take as an analytic patient a person toward whom one feels little or nothing; a person toward whom one's response is flat and unmoved. Analysts use their emotional responses as a major source of their empathic linkage to analysands' inner feelings. Combined with intellectual knowledge, the analyst's own emotional reactions provide information from which to deduce many of the subtle nuances of the analysand's communications. These feeling responses are thus a part of the analyst's tools for "listening" or resonating with the patient.

During the long process of the analytic work, the analyst listens back and forth between the patient's associations and his or her own responses, much as one might listen to a musical performance. The finest range of the analyst's appreciation of subtleties often occurs when the tempo within the analysis is lively but steady. In periods of prolonged dragginess, attentiveness may lapse. On the other hand, in periods of excitability, nuances may be lost as the analysis deals with a sense of overload or impelling immediacy. The teacher I mentioned described a patient (not in analysis) whose belligerence presented a constant explosive possibility. As a therapist, he told this patient, he could not do his best work when the hackles on the back of his neck were raised. Within the extremes noted here, however, the experienced analyst is able to work effectively and comfortably with a broad range of people.

The Prospective Analysand's Assessment

Earlier we looked at the question: "How do I find the psyoanalyst I want?" During a consultation this may take the form: "How can I tell if this analyst is the right one for me?" The consultation provides an opportunity for you to gain an evaluative impression of the analyst. Sometimes, especially if the person is acutely troubled, what is most important is the reassurance that, with the analyst's help, relief is possible. Other people come with a conscious plan to look the analyst over, and this may be a particular concern if the person has previously had an unproductive experience with treatment. Some people make appointments with more than one analyst and use their experiences for fruitful comparison. Others may seemingly ineffectively "shop around." Obviously, if a person is unusually fearful or unusually demanding, this may add to the problems of finding an analyst.

What about questions concerning the analyst's personal inclinations and values? Beyond a polite acknowledging response, the analyst is unlikely to say much. The kind of information the analyst gives concerns analysis in general and arrangements about time, fees, etc. The reason for this is often difficult to understand. If the analyst were to comply to demands to furnish personal information, to voice his or her attitudes about politics, marriage, civil rights, women's liberation, and so on, this would jeopardize the treatment.

The question "What do analysts reveal about themselves?" requires a complicated answer. In the consultation and especially during the analysis, analysts constantly reveal to their analysands where they stand in one quite circumscribed but all-important area—how they function as analysts—through what they select out of the analysands' associations to ask about, comment on, or interpret. In addition, analysts continually reveal to their analysands information about themselves that seems inadvertent to the analysis but can become a useful component. Here I have in mind the analyst's gender, accent, age, appearance, clothing, office decor, comings and goings, etc., which may stimulate fantasies on the analysand's part. There is an apparent paradox: If analysands can weave any information about the analyst into associations that can help move the analysis forward, why don't analysts answer questions about themselves? One answer is that it is often easier for analysands to recognize the largely self-created fantasy-like origins of references to the analyst if they are speculating rather than working with known facts. The analysand also may feel freer to express thoughts and feelings about the analyst if it is understood they reflect the analysand's subjective picture. But the main reason lies in another direction. The focus of analysis is on the *analysand's inner world*. It is the "analyst" *in* the analysand's inner world that both are interested in knowing about. Anything that would shift focus from that opposes one of the main approaches by which the treatment works.

My advice to a person going for a consultation is: Try to prepare yourself for a mutual exchange. Present yourself, your way of relating, and your problems as straightforwardly as you can. In this way you will provide meaningful information that will help the consulting analyst give the best recommendation that he or she can. At the same time you can try to be aware of the analyst's contribution. Does this analyst seem understanding, both emotionally and intellectually? Does his or her manner seem to facilitate your communicating or at least not make it more difficult? I don't mean that you need to particularize your reactions in any formal fashion. It's more a kind of intuitive sensing: "This analyst gives me the feeling he knows what he is doing and I think I can work with him."

In addition to your general appraisal, you may have a variety of "low-key" reactions that are a part of any meeting—professional or social. You may feel: "I like the way she smiles" or "I felt irritated when he interrupted me to ask a question." These "minor" reactions are important and may well be recalled later during the analysis, when an understanding of their meanings may provide valuable insight. They do not constitute the basis of a personality incompatibility. It is only when the reactions are major—when you have a very strong emotional response—that you need to beware of a possible incompatibility. If, for instance, you experience an overwhelming erotic attraction to a particular analyst or find the analyst's reactions unduly abrasive or eccentric, you may decide against working with that analyst and seek consultation with another.

In trying to help friends and colleagues assess their reactions to an analyst after a consultation, the question I have found most helpful is: "Did he or she seem 'professional'?" In their way of relating to prospective analysands, analysts should convey that they are genuinely interested in their work, honest and ethical in their dealings, practical in their arrangements, and humanistically concerned in their outlook. This is what I mean by "professional." The prospective analysand who can answer my question affirmatively can reasonably conclude that the potential for a good fit exists and that analyst and analysand will be able together to do the work of analysis.

5 The Couch and Free Association

The moment of seriously asking yourself, "Is psychoanalysis for me?," is like a point on a trip where you find yourself at a crossroads. How to decide to proceed? Should you continue on the same bumpy road? Or take another, one that might be more fulfilling? The prudent traveler draws together all the available information about the possible new road and tries to assess whether this route will fit his or her needs and wishes.

In asking yourself about psychoanalysis, the first image to come to mind might well be the familiar stereotype of a patient lying on a couch and, sitting behind, a cartoon character of a little, bearded man mumbling something in a Viennese accent. How accurate is this picture? Psychoanalysis does involve a patient (the analysand) on a couch with an analyst seated behind. But obviously analysts come in all sizes, with or without beards, male or female, with or without foreign accents.

What other stereotypes might you have encountered? Perhaps you've heard that the analysand is supposed to say whatever comes to mind. That much is accurate. However, in comical depictions, the person is shown chattering away with a cartoon bubble that never ends. Free association is rarely that easy, as we shall see. Still, it may sound appealing to be able to voice all one's innermost thoughts to another human being who listens attentively, without making judgments. Let's explore the stereotypes a little more.

HOW DOES IT FEEL TO USE THE COUCH?

The idea of lying on the couch may give rise to a lot of different feelings. In one view, lying on the couch may seem a welcome respite from the pressures of daily life, a chance to relax your body and, to some degree, your mind. There you are, free of routine concerns, thinking imaginatively, speaking without inhibition, engaged in a kind of soliloquy. On the other hand, using the couch may seem threatening in its strangeness. How can you feel safe conversing with someone you can't see? You won't be able to observe the other person's reaction, note the expression on his or her face, read approval or disapproval, encouragement or discouragement. Indeed, it may seem quite frightening not to have access to all those signs from the person's appearance and body responses that tell one how one's words are being received. None of the normal "security checks" is available.

Both the eager anticipation and the fear are normal responses to the couch, and the same person may experience both. On the one hand, it may seem that without a chance to gauge the other person's reactions, you'll be freer to talk. But, then, how can you tell if your worst fears are true? Lying down is certainly attractive as a way of gaining comfort and relief from the rigors of day-to-day life. But isn't there a danger of becoming childlike, feeling dependent and coddled? Aren't you more vulnerable when you're lying down, with fewer means of escape?

I don't have ready answers to all these questions about the couch. Often the reactions to the couch provide a starting point for the analytic inquiry—a chance to explore both your hopes and fears. In allaying any apprehensions, it may be helpful to remember that the use of the couch is merely the means for creating the setting in which the essential communication between analysand and analyst takes place. It is neither a trick nor a magical device. It is simply a tool for facilitating the important work of psychoanalysis. Free association is another, different kind of tool—a basic working principle.

WHAT IS FREE ASSOCIATION LIKE?

The idea that the analysand should say whatever comes into his or her mind lies at the core of psychoanalytic treatment. Early on, Freud discovered that thinking is a continuous process; the translation of thought into speech, however, does not yield an exact replica of the thought, but rather a reproduction of the thought after it has passed through some censoring or correcting or monitoring. In social and business conversation, and even in very intimate conversation, we say as much as possible what we *wish* to mean. Yet often what we wish to convey is not what we spontaneously think. As Freud discovered, much can be learned if the analyst and analysand can look at both what the analysand would choose to say *and* the thoughts he or she would prefer to restrict, correct, or alter. It is the latter thoughts that tell a great deal about what we are less aware of and yet are thinking and feeling all the time. Our spontaneous thinking, our inner speech, has more to do with out secret self—secret not only from others but often also from ourselves, in that we may hide its implications from ourselves. Thus, Freud established the "basic rule" that the analysand should say whatever comes to mind, without censoring, restricting, or altering what he or she spontaneously thinks and feels. In other words, the analysand tries to put the spontaneous flow of thoughts and feelings, his or her stream of consciousness, into words which are communicated to the analyst.

On first hearing about this basic rule, a person may say: "Well, if that's what I have to do to get well or to gain the understanding I wish to gain, I'll do it. It doesn't seem so difficult; in fact, it seems little enough compared with what other doctors might prescribe. It's not like having to undergo an operation, perform difficult exercises, or follow a strict diet." Yet, as I've already hinted, it's not so easy to free-associate as it may seem. Why not try an experiment? Try to follow the basic rule aloud in the privacy of your room. Do you notice that before long you're involved in a process of selecting? As you put some of your thoughts and feelings into words, do you leave some others out? You may object: "But I think faster than I can speak and, besides, there is no way to put my thoughts and feelings into words without making sentences, and sometimes I don't think in whole sentences."

Before long, any person trying to follow the basic rule of psychoanalysis discovers unforeseen obstacles. And there's another catch. Even if one conscientiously put into words all one's *thoughts*, one might leave out an equally important part of the communication—one's feelings. Then, if one concentrated on describing one's feelings, one might get so involved in the emotion that one pushed aside certain thoughts. Or one might work oneself into an emotional state where one lost all capacity for self-reflective awareness. By now you may be despairing. Is it possible to carry out this rule?

Because, for the beginning analysand, the task of putting all thoughts and feelings into words is so difficult, I ask the analysand to follow a general working *principle* rather than a basic *rule*. Sharing a working principle rather than obeying a rule is less likely to arouse feelings of failure or guilt for noncompliance or to provoke rebellious resistance. To the extent analysands do communicate using this principle, following it successfully, they know they are working *with* the analyst toward a common end. When they cannot or will not follow the principle, they come to recognize that they are making choices (consciously or unconsciously) that must be understood and worked out or there will be limitations to what they can expect to accomplish.

As we look further into how this basic working principle operates, we encounter additional pitfalls. There are many ways of trying to shortchange the rule. One person may rationalize that since the *rule* is to say whatever comes into his mind as he talks to the analyst, he can remain in nominal compliance but retain his "secrets" by not permitting himself to think about a particular disturbing subject during the session. All analysands, even highly motivated ones, use this exclusion clause to eliminate the basic rule as a *rule* at some time or another. Another analysand may dutifully follow the *rule* as rule, reporting what she brings to mind during the hour, yet unknowingly keeping a whole area of significance excluded from consciousness during any analytic session. In other words, this person has arranged not to know that she is censoring or suppressing something. Admittedly, on the face of it, she *is* trying to follow the rule. But it will not "work" that way.

Given all the escape routes, many analysts add some qualifications to their description of the rule. I ask analysands not only to say what comes into their minds, but to let themselves be as free as they possibly can to think and feel about everything that has personal meaning to them. They should try to be open to any thoughts about events, plans, or people, past, present, or future. And not only should they express these thoughts, but they should communicate their emotional reactions. Beyond that, they should note any body sensations, such as a tensing of the shoulders or a tightness in the throat. Even more, they should voice any thoughts or feelings about the person to whom they are speaking—the analyst.

That's a tall order! Indeed, it may sound frightening. You may wonder: "What if I don't want to tell you certain of my thoughts and feelings? What if I think you are restless and not listening to me?" Or if I think you're angry and fed up with me? How do I handle that?" Each person will handle it differently. Some analysands avoid the "burden" of free association as long as possible and only gradually come to grips with it. Others force themselves to bravely acknowledge their reluctance from the first and plunge headlong into the most difficult things they can think of to say. Others try to struggle with this task, recognizing its difficulties and sharing that recognition, and often getting some understanding and help as they struggle with it. In no case does a new analysand find it easy. It may, however, be encouraging to remember that in the very struggle to try to work within the basic principle, many insights important to analytic progress occur.

WHAT ABOUT THE ADVICE TO MAKE NO MAJOR DECISIONS WHILE IN PSYCHOANALYSIS?

You may have heard of the recommendation that an analysand make no major life decisions while in analysis. For many years this rule was stated in just those words. Today, however, few analysts present this as a condition for beginning analysis, primarily because it no longer seems as reasonable as when it was originally made.

In the earliest days, the length of an analysis varied from three months to a little over a year. Under such circumstances it was no particular hardship for people to accept the recommendation that they make no major decisions. But today an analysis usually takes a good deal longer. The idea that one should not marry, have a child, buy a house, or change jobs for an extended number of years is incompatible with normal expectations. To accomplish one or more of these changes may be precisely one's purpose in seeking analysis. The "no major decisions while in analysis" rule thus might paralyze analytic movement toward greater freedom to act in accord with inner needs and values.

When people ask me about this rule, I tell them that I have no specific rule excluding major decisions, that my one "rule" is the basic working principle. If they think about this basic working principle, it should be clear that any major decision would have to come into their awareness and thus inevitably become a part of the analytic work. They would need to look at it, associate about it, evaluate it, and challenge it in the same way they would an anxiety, a dream, a slip, a memory, or any other thought or feeling. It would be contradictory to the general goal and objective of analysis for an analysand to formulate and act on a major decision without having subjected that decision to a thorough analysis, with attention to its meaning and implications, both as a conscious plan and as an issue with links to past events and unconscious determinants. Otherwise the decision might serve as a screen, obscuring the very conflicts the person is seeking to understand.

6

The Analytic "Contract"

At this point you may well be wondering about the analyst's role in all this. What does he or she do? And you may also have questions about the practical arrangements. How often do you have to come? How much does it cost? How long will it take?

THE ANALYST'S TASK

After the general evaluation of the person's problems and suitability for analysis, there is usually a discussion of the mutual requirements of the participants. It is at this point that I bring up the basic working principle, which we've just discussed. I also describe the other side of the working principle—my response to the analysand's effort to follow it. I try to convey in a few words the special kind of attentiveness the analyst provides: "I will listen carefully to your associations. Sometimes I may intervene very little. Other times I may respond more frequently. I may ask questions to help you bring out information or to recognize ambiguities. I may make comments that will help you to observe difficulties or successes you are having in following the basic principle. I may note possible connections between one group of your associations and another." All this is but an introduction. The nature of the analyst's contributions becomes clearer during the course of the analysis, as we shall see in later chapters.

Often, however, in the consultation interview, people have additional questions about the analyst-analysand interaction I have just sketched in. A common question in my experience is one that in some way expresses a fear that the analyst will remain silent and unresponsive, with the analysand left lying on the couch, deprived of eye contact and further deprived of verbal connectedness. I believe each prospective analysand needs to be reassured that such a dreary picture of coldness and abandonment couldn't be the design of the analytic method. Although the analyst may at times be silent or even seem unresponsive, there should be a *basic sense* that one is talking to a concerned, caring therapist. Episodic feelings of loneliness or of isolation can then be analyzed within the general context of two people working together to understand.

Another question that often comes up is this: "I've heard that once the analysis begins I won't be able to ask you questions. Is that so?" Here, again, an explanation may help. Leaving aside necessary questions about time and fee arrangements, vacations, and the like, the analyst does not as a general rule answer questions that arise within the hour. Often the analyst will treat a question as an association, for which the analysand has chosen the interrogative form of speech. From that position, the analyst will respond to it as to any association. He or she may listen further or inquire about the analysand's choice in expressing this thought as a question. For instance, is putting forth a thought as a question more comfortable than expressing the same idea as a declarative statement? The analyst may note an underlying curiosity in the question and suggest the person associate further to that. Or the analyst may observe that the question itself reflects the person's putting together a number of issues, much as the analyst's own summing-up questions do. In this case the analyst may encourage the analysand to take up his or her own question as a source for further reflective inquiry. In all these possible responses, the analyst is purposively trying to further the analytic work. It may be difficult to appreciate this point, for under ordinary social conventions not responding informatively to a question is seen as rude and insensitive. But psychoanalysis does not deal in ordinary information. The aim is to understand how the analysand thinks and feels—not to supply ready answers, however frustrating this may be.

The Need for Continuity

Now let's turn to some of the formal arrangements for psychoanalysis. Most analysts agree that the optimal arrangement is for the analysand to come for four or five sessions per week for forty-five or fifty minutes duration. Personally I prefer to work five times per week for fifty-minute sessions. I may, however, based on the exigencies of my schedule or the analysand's, recommend a four-day-a-week schedule to begin with.

Is this frequency necessary? The four- or five-day-a-week schedule is based on empirical evidence that it works best. Analysts have found that what the analysand keeps out of awareness is elusive; the four- or five-day-a-week framework allows both analysand and analyst to remain close to the "unconscious." In the early days of psychoanalysis, analysts not uncommonly scheduled hours six days a week. At that time the analytic effort was directed much more toward the analysis of symptoms and lasted a far shorter length of time—sometimes only for several months. Today, when analyses are directed to the understanding and resolution of conflicts and their antecedents in all sectors of the personality, the length of time is reckoned in years not months. Because of the duration over years, most analysts believe that more than five hours per week interferes with the optimal balance between the analysand's (and the analyst's) commitment to analysis and to involvement with family, work, and recreational pursuits.

Although pressure from either the analysand or analyst for an overcommitment to analysis rarely occurs, pressure for an undercommitment is not uncommon. The tempo of our society is a fast one: "Time is money. Money talks." These clichés express a reality about the demands of daily life. Thus it is natural that a person, confronted with the recommendation that he take four or five hours plus travel time out of his already busy life, may plead "Can't it be less—three, maybe?" My answer is "no." If one is to give analysis the best chance to be effective, a minimum of four sessions is needed. An explanation of why the continuity is so critical would require an understanding of the whole process in depth, and as I describe the analytic experience in more detail, I hope the need for frequent sessions will become more apparent. When this issue comes up in consultation, I usually refer the person back to our consideration of the basic working principle. I explain that the state of mind in which the most productive free association occurs is a fragile one, dependent on the delicate working relationship that the analyst and analysand establish. This state of mind is best activated when frequent contact allows a partial carrying over of thoughts from hour to hour, although it can be reestablished after a break if the break is not too long. The combination of breaks within the week (when there are less than four meetings) plus breaks over the weekend operates to mute or dampen the emotional connectedness of the analysand to the associative work and to the relationship with the analyst.

WORKING OUT THE TIME

Once the prospective analysand accepts that four or five hours are required, we begin to try to work out the arrangements. At this point the time commitments of two people have to be meshed. Naturally this can be best accomplished if a spirit of mutual cooperativeness exists. I usually ask the person about his or her time possibilities, keeping in mind what my own schedule will permit. Analysts work on varied schedules. Some begin early in the morning (6:00 A.M.), others work in the evenings. Most have other activities—hospital affiliations; training, lecturing, and supervisory tasks; consulting for courts and governmental agencies—which take time away from their office hours. And of course analysand's time availability also varies. As a broad generalization, most analysts have sessions scheduled from approximately 7:30 A.M. to 6:30 P.M. My experience is that the early hours, the last hours, and the hours near to the lunchbreak are most in demand.

Many employed people express an understandable initial reluctance to come during the workday. It isn't so much the interference with their work (a matter that few raise and most believe they can compensate for); the reluctance has more to do with disclosure. To leave work regularly at a fixed time inevitably evokes curiosity. Moreover, it may require at the outset an acknowledgment to the employer in order to gain permission. Many prospective analysands fear the employer's reaction. The employer might think less of them, categorize them as a neurotic, with adverse effects on their employment. They also fear the censure or condescension of their fellow employees. It would be naive to believe that these dreaded, hurtful responses do not occur. Yet in my experience they occur far less often and to a far less hurtful degree than most people fear. On the one hand, the existence of difficulties in coping is widespread, bringing a large measure of compassion. On the other hand, the people the prospective analysand works with and for are usually already aware of tensions, problems, and symptoms he or she is struggling with. In that instance, nothing really hidden or private is being disclosed by the person's entering treatment.

ARRANGING THE FEE

Many people who are contemplating psychoanalysis use other sources to get information about fees beforehand. My policy is to ask the prospective analysands what information they have and what their expectations are. If their information is accurate, I am able to confirm their research. If their information is false, I am alerted to possible emotional meanings of a fee lower or higher than the one they expect. Once the person has answered my question, I will tell him or her my standard fee per session. Some people accept this fee without further discussion; others evidence any number of emotional reactions from relief ("It might have been more") to dismay ("How can I afford it").

Fees vary more than any other arrangement for analysis. The most pronounced variance is between areas rather than within an area. At the time of this writing, for instance, average fees in Los Angeles, Houston, and Chicago are higher than those in Baltimore or Washington, D.C. Within each area, there are also variances, but most analysts with the same years of experience and professional reputation in a given area will charge roughly the same standard fee.

The term "standard fee" refers to the usual or customary charge the analyst makes for the offered service. The same practice is found in medicine: a surgeon customarily charges a particular amount for a procedure like an appendectomy or an internist for a complete physical exam. Unlike the charge that is based on a service as such, however, the analytic fee is based on a service per fixed unit of time. Two factors, then, help to determine the fee: the ordinary marketplace pressures of supply and demand and the availability and limitations of time. Inflation is a marketplace factor that has accounted for the rate of rise of fees—doubling between 1969 and 1979. As has been traditional in medicine, higher fees may at times be charged for those who are relatively wealthy, with somewhat lower fees for those who require a reduced fee to afford the treatment. The standard fee for a given analyst might be the average of these adjustments.

In my experience many fair-minded people have differing views about analytic fees. From one view, the expense, especially over a year, is staggering. Looked at this way, the question logically rises—why does the analyst charge so much? Beyond the general issue of why so many commodities and services cost so much, the specific answer about analytic charges lies in the fact that each analysand receives a substantial percentage of the time the analyst has available—or more properly, of the care that analyst can provide because of the time needed for the analytic process to unfold successfully.

Is analysis, then, only for rich people? The charge has been levied that analysis is an elitest treatment. "If "elitest" means it is a treatment limited to a small group of rich people, then the facts don't bear this out. Analysis is sought by and available to those who earn from the middle-income level upward and, at times, by special arrangement, to those whose earnings are less. This is made possible by a number of factors. Many analysands have insurance plans that pay varying percentages of the analytic fee. In addition, the income tax deductions for treatment and travel costs may make it more affordable.

As noted, reduced fee arrangements are at times available. Many analysts see analysands at varying amounts less than their standard fee. Many psychoanalytic societies have facilities for screening and referring prospective analysands. Those who can afford minimal fees can be treated by psychoanalysts-in-training. In these cases the training institute assumes the responsibility for overseeing the quality of the analytic experience, with appropriate supervision of the psychoanalyst-in-training's therapeutic work. In some instances grants from the government and philanthropic organizations have assisted in making low-fee psychoanalysis possible.

In the consultative interview, the discussion about the fee generally evolves in a natural progression. As the prospective analysand reveals a great deal of personal information, the analyst learns many facts about the person's work, background, family responsibilities, and prospects. The analyst thus gains a general sense of socioeconomic status. Beyond this, however, analyst and prospective analysand may need to begin the practice of direct inquiry and response that will prove crucial during the analysis. The social convention of euphemistic references to money has to be discarded. To properly evaluate the best practical arrangements to recommend, the analyst may ask the person about earned income, insurance coverage, savings, other available sources of revenue, debts and liabilities, as well as prospects in the near and distant future. Often people are reticent in revealing these facts. However much the analyst may understand this hesitation, he or she must persist—both to gain the information needed to set the fee and to encourage the person to begin to reveal frankly private thoughts and feelings. On the basis of the information received, the analyst may decide the person can afford the standard fee or that a modification is indicated. The analyst will then indicate the specific amount. If, after considering his or her finances, the person agrees to the amount set, they can consider the fee to be a mutually arrived at part of the analytic "contract." Changes would require mutual reconsideration and renewed agreement.

HOLIDAYS, VACATIONS, MISSED APPOINTMENTS

At this point in the interview I usually offer additional information on the subject of scheduling. I mention my usual holidays: in my case this involves my not working on the major holidays (Washington's Birthday, July 4th, Labor Day, Thanksgiving,

Christmas, and New Year's Day), two Jewish holy days, and during the time of professional meetings in December and May. I also explain that I usually take five or six weeks of vacation, three or four weeks in August, the rest at other times. I indicate that I will tell the analysand the dates of my vacation as many months in advance as I can, and recommend that, if at all possible, in order to preserve maximum continuity, the person should try to coordinate his or her vacation with mine.

Another practical issue I bring up at this point is the handling of charges for missed appointments. Analysts vary in their approach to this feature of the arrangements. My practice, which I arrived at after trying many different procedures, is to inform analysands they will be billed for appointments they miss. The exception is that if I know in advance and can fill the hour, I will do so and not bill the person. In the case of hazardous weather conditions, I do not expect someone to attempt to come and do not bill for the missed hour. If a person has a conflict with a particular hour, I am as flexible as I can be in arranging an alternative appointment within the same day or week to preserve optimal continuity.

Many of my colleagues follow a different practice in charging for missed appointments. Some charge for all missed appointments. Others specify that if patients are ill or must be away because of business requirements, they will not be charged. Still others don't charge at all for missed appointments. I believe there are advantages and disadvantages to each of these positions. A disadvantage in charging regularly is that it may falsely convey or actually constitute a rigidity or greediness on the analyst's part. Yet charging for some reasons and not for others may put the analyst in a judgmental position, falsely conveying or actually reflecting moral values. Not charging for any missed appointments may convey a permissive looseness or result in a diminished investment in the continuity of the analytic process. The important consideration is whether the chosen practice allows the analyst to best perform the analytic task. If the analyst honestly believes the arrangements permit him or her to establish a basic working alliance, then the analysand's reactions to the specific choice become part of the meaningful exchange of the analysis—the exchange that gives analysis life and immediacy as a shared exploration by two involved people.

RENEGOTIATING THE CONTRACT

In discussing the arrangements about hours and fees, I try to convey to the prospective analysand that we are aiming for an agreement that is acceded to mutually. We arrive at it differently, of course. I set my own fee, and the hours I offer are set by the requirements of my schedule. A person may ask for and receive an adjustment—a different hour or an altered fee. Once we arrive at the starting arrangements, they can be regarded as an agreed-to, shared responsibility rather than an autocratic, arbitrary assignment by the analyst to a compliant and potentially resentful analysand. Thus I regard changes as necessitating a "renegotiation" of the contract. Working out a change in the appointment schedule, for instance, requires a reconsideration of the practical needs of each partner. Fees too can be altered. Certainly, given the fluctuations in today's general economy, this is logically to be expected. Moreover, the analyand's circumstances may change. When a fee is renegotiated during the analysis, it is necessary that the basis for the reconsideration be understood in order that analyst and analysand retain a sense of a mutual sharing in the basic arrangements. This frequently involves investigation of hidden meanings through the use of the analytic method, as well as a discussion of the overt pragmatic considerations.

HOW LONG DOES ANALYSIS TAKE?

The question "How long does analysis take?" invariably comes up. This question is almost impossible to answer satisfactorily. A statistical answer—for instance, "Based on X hundreds or thousands of cases treated in the last decade, the average analysis took X years, months, and days"—conveys only an impersonal number. It does not reveal either the quality of the results or the kind of patient being treated. The real question the prospective analysand has in mind is: "How long will *my* analysis take to achieve the results I hope for?" And this is a question the analyst can't answer. Will further knowledge of the person over time cause the analyst to alter the diagnostic impression? Will the analysand show greater or less facility with the analytic method than estimated? Will external circumstances work to facilitate or complicate analytic progress? These factors are all unknowns. Nonetheless, the prospective analysand needs some kind of guidance. The best answer I can offer is this: It is rare in my experience for a successful analysis to be completed in less than four years, although it is common for an analysis that shows little promise to be interrupted before four years. Six years is probably the average time for a successful analysis, but *many* successful analyses take longer. Some ultimately highly successful analyses have taken ten years or more.

There are many difficulties in answering the question about length of time. It isn't simply that the analyst doesn't know. Whatever answer the analyst offers may lead to immediate or ultimate distress for the analysand. The thought of ten years may give rise to instant alarm or discouragement. Four years, however, may be heard as the equivalent of a promise—in four years you will graduate. If the analysand weaves this statement of time into his or her pattern of collective achievements, frustration may ensue if the expectation is not met. All these reactions become part of the content of the analysis, but in the beginning they may indeed detract from clearheadedness in making a decision to undertake analysis. My best answer is that analysis is a treatment that deals with the individuality of the analysand. Thus, no one can predict the individual's progress or its rate beyond an optimistic and yet realistic assessment of potential.

7
Decisions, Decisions

"I've gone through the consultation interviews and psycho-analysis was recommended. Now what do I do? Is psychoanaly-sis really what I want and need? Will the gains be worth the sacrifices? How on earth do I arrive at a decision? It sounds like a big undertaking. Will it work for me? Will it help?"

Understanding the reasoning behind the analyst's recom-mendation that psychoanalysis is the treatment of choice in-volves different problems for different people. One woman, knowledgeable about psychoanalysis, had psychoanalysis in mind before the consultation and chose to consult a psychoan-alyst she hoped would be available to treat her. For her, the analyst's recommendation was a confirmation of her own opin-ion, an acceptance of her personal suitability, and a general relief. Another person, minimally knowledgeable about differ-ent treatment methods, simply went to talk with an expert about his difficulties in coping. It came as a relief that the ana-lyst believed he could be helped. And he even accepted the idea of a kind of treatment that would enable him to discover, com-prehend, and master unconscious emotional conflicts that under-lay his difficulties. But he was startled by the investment in time and money the treatment entailed, especially the length of time it would take. He was also perplexed about the whole process of free association, the couch, and the conceptualization of how his problem would be dealt with that was outlined to him.

For both prospective analysands, it was puzzling that after one, two, or three relatively brief contacts the analytic consultant could make so far-reaching an assessment. Looking back at this puzzlement, Mr. Brown said that at the time he felt unsure my recommendation was based on a careful diagnosis of his problems and a disinterested evaluation of psychoanalysis as the best possible treatment for him. He worried that, being an analyst, I had recommended analysis so that I could get to do what I liked and was trained to do, much as he feared that an architect would build, a surgeon cut, a lawyer sue. At the point in his analysis that he brought this issue up, Mr. Brown was himself beginning to realize the full import of the problems he had described in the initial interviews. To the analyst, his presenting problems had indicated underlying tensions and conflicts. Mr. Brown, however, had been more focused on the immediate issue and thus had not perceived this so clearly.

A critical factor in determining the analyst's recommendation for analysis is how motivated to make significant changes the person appears to be. This criterion is especially important when the analyst believes that, because of the nature of the problems and their persistence, the analysis will be long and difficult. Major personality changes do not come easily. Superficially adaptive, temporary pleasure-giving or tension-relieving patterns, which in the long run are self-defeating, may be clung to with the tenacity of a life-or-death struggle. A strong basic motivation to change is needed to persist and "win" the battle.

It has been stated that the ideal prospect for psychoanalysis is someone who is sick enough to want it and well enough to tolerate it. This aphorism addresses both the suffering that motivates the analysand and the willingness to trust, relatedness, and general functional ability that the method requires of the analysand if it is to succeed. How does the consulting analyst evaluate the "well-enough" side? In the consultation one person may reveal conflicts with people involving hostility, suspiciousness, or marked emotional restrictiveness. The analyst must then assess whether this person's limitations in forming relationships are tempered by enough "basic trust" to form a working alliance with the analyst. Another individual may have difficulties in accepting responsibility, keeping appointments, and handling finances. Does this person show the potential to control the more self-destructive manifestations of these tendencies, to keep closely enough to the analytic appointment and fee arrangements, and to maintain a generally functional life pattern, so that the analysis can take hold? Overall, the consulting analyst must conclude that there is a high probability the prospective analysand will attempt to live up to his or her side of the therapeutic responsibility—to maintain an open, honest communication with the analyst and be reasonably protective of the practical framework of the treatment. If this is the case, the analyst may recommend analysis, with the assumption that any problems that arise will be "grist for the analytic mill"—that is, they will provide material for analytic investigation, with the aim of analytic understanding and resolution.

QUESTIONS FOR REFLECTION

Is the Method for You?

In attempting to decide whether to follow the recommendation for analysis, I believe you should first try to sense: how well does the method seem to "fit"? This may seem like an impossible task—the matching of one unknown with another. But it's more a matter of imagination. At some level, whether conscious or partly conscious, you've probably been trying on the role of analysand for size. You may even have begun long before the consultative interviews. In that case the consultation may have served to fill in gaps in the imaginary experience. The analyst now has a face and a manner of speaking and relating, the couch a shape and color, the arrangements a detailed form. Most important, the method has been reviewed.

Perhaps, as the basic working principle of free association was discussed, you "tried it out"—mentally placing yourself on the couch and attempting to voice your thoughts and feelings. Does this feel possible? More or less comfortable? One prospective analysand might reflect: "I've always wanted to have a trust-worthy person in whom to confide. For years I've longed to speak to somebody about my inner feelings. And here's some-body without bias, somebody bound by his profession to protect my privacy. What I say to him will be confidential. His first responsibility is to me—not to my family or my wife or anyone else. That's important. With his help, I think I can learn what I need to know to get myself together the way I want to be."

Another person, especially someone who did not expect psychoanalysis to be recommended, might be more ambivalent: "I'm certainly pleased that this analyst thinks she can help me, but I'm not so sure about this kind of treatment. Lying on the couch seems strange. Maybe after a few weeks I won't have anything more to say. There are things about my family I've never told anybody. It might be good to get them off my chest, but it still seems risky. And what about sex? Is it fair to my wife to talk about our problems? I know this woman's a therapist—she's not supposed to judge me, but can anybody not judge another person? She seemed to listen in a fair-minded way and I like the understanding way in which she responded. But how will it feel if I can't see her? It's such an amazing proposition—beginning psychoanalysis. I've heard criticisms from some friends and good comments from others. Perhaps I really should give it a try—it does seem to offer the most. If I find it isn't for me, I can always quit. But I am going to try to make it work."

Are the Arrangements Comfortable Enough?

In reflecting on time and money arrangements, the prospective analysand may be on more familiar, although not necessarily smoother ground. Take Mr. Hill. He's been considering psychoanalysis in his mind for a while and has, in some sense, prepared himself. After the first consultation he checked back with his boss, who said it would be all right for him to come in an hour late Monday and Thursday and to be out for a longer lunch hour Tuesday and Wednesday. The Friday hour, however, seems more difficult because that's when they have their weekly closing meeting. Thinking it over, Mr. Hill tells himself: "The doctor said if I can't arrange it now we could start with four sessions and add the fifth later when he gets an early hour on Friday. I told the boss I'd make up the time, but he didn't seem too concerned. He said as long as my work doesn't suffer it's okay. I've checked out my money. Sure, it'll put a dent in our available funds and use up some of our savings, but I can manage it. There's one thing I don't like—the August vacation. Still, if that's when he goes away, maybe I'll try it. The kids are always urging me to go to the beach then anyway."

For another person the practical arrangements may be more problematic. Mrs. Pevsner, for instance, kept going back and forth: "I don't know how I'm going to work out this whole analysis business. I want it, I need it, but I just don't see how. Wednesday and Thursday at 11:00 is all right because the kids are at school then, and I don't really have a fixed schedule for my freelance work. But 3 P.M. the other days—that means I have to get an afternoon sitter, and I don't know if high school students are out early enough. Besides, sitters mean extra money. I had better take that out of my earnings because Bill [her husband] is angry enough about my hiring someone to clean the house. Still, I'll have to ask him for some of the money to pay for analysis. If we were getting along better that would be easier. Of course, if we got along better, maybe I wouldn't need analysis. No, that's not fair. I've had problems for years, even before our marriage. I just have to find the money. I hate to tell anybody in my family; I can imagine what they'll say. Maybe, though, I should ask mother for a loan against my inheritance. She won't like it, but she'll do it. We could also dig into our savings—at least until I'm working more or Bill's raise comes through. That's what savings are for, I guess. I have to look at it as an investment in the future. If analysis helps to save our marriage, it will be worth it."

What Are the Alternatives?

Earlier, I mentioned the consideration of treatment methods other than psychoanalysis. Often the psychoanalyst who recommends analysis also treats patients by other means, most commonly individual psychotherapy or group therapy. Other available methods include marriage counseling, family therapy, sexual therapy, biofeedback, behavior modification, hypnotherapy, "expressive" therapies like "primal scream," encounter groups, and transcendental meditation. Frequently, prospective analysands have already tried one or more of these other methods, most commonly psychotherapy.

How, before trying it, can you evaluate if analysis is best for your individual needs? Obviously this is a difficult question. Although the analyst's recommendation is an important guide, you too must be convinced that analysis will really help. One woman, for instance, had already been in psychotherapy. Now she was considering analysis. "I know psychotherapy and psychoanalysis are both treatments in which I work with a therapist to understand more about myself and my problems," she reflected. "In my two years of psychotherapy I did learn a lot and I'm not so afraid of closeness now. My airplane phobia got better for a time, but then it got worse again. I never did understand why. My therapist kept indicating that in twice-a-week psychotherapy we could get into many of the problems, but not deeply and persistently enough to get to the bottom of them. I keep thinking of how grandmother's death affected me—the way dad got depressed and mom got impatient with him and more involved with me. It seems real important. I talked about it in psychotherapy and, sure, that helped, but I still don't understand just what it has to do with things I feel now. Because of the time and the money I'm tempted to go back into psychotherapy, but Dr. Lester [the analyst] said in the long run it might take longer and I'd get less out of it. Whenever I've really tried to go into a problem fully, I've felt better about myself. Maybe this will be the same. I know in analysis I'll have the chance to follow through on my grandmother's death in a way I couldn't if I went back into psychotherapy."

In some ways, weighing the benefits of psychoanalysis versus psychotherapy is easier, for they have much in common. Other methods may be so different from analysis that comparisons are difficult. Unfortunately, there is no laboratory for the mind where one can send a culture of the patient's bacteria and observe which antibiotic works best as a therapeutic agent. Nor is there enough standardization of diagnosis and technique to allow two different procedures to be tested in statistically significant numbers and compared in terms of efficacy. Such studies depend, for their validity, on the replication of the same "case" in a number of different samples. But, with emotional difficulties, each person's "case" is very individual.

It might be helpful to review at this point what psychoanalysis is. The plan is to conduct a thorough investigation into the nature and origins of an individual's emotional problems. Analyst and analysand seek insight into the pulls and tugs of conflicts—conscious and especially unconscious—that affect what the person chooses to do. Both seek to understand alterations in the way the analysand senses him- or herself and others. Why, for instance, might the analysand at times feel empty and unfulfilled, without purpose or direction? Have frightening, aversive, unempathic experiences in the past left the analysand vulnerable? Do present situations trigger responses by which the analysand protects him- or herself against these vulnerabilities to distress? Both analyst and analysand try to look at the analysand's current patterns of response to stress to see if they have grown out of the child's rigid, often ineffective efforts to cope. By becoming aware of the part past experience plays in the present, all phases of life—infancy, childhood, adolescence, and adulthood—can be integrated into a more harmonious sense of self. Capacities that have remained inaccessible or been "lost" can be recovered, developed, and stabilized. As we shall see, the progress of analysis itself takes on a kind of cohesive development, with a beginning, a middle, and an end. It moves purposefully toward insight, personality change, and resolution of conflicts, and then by mutual agreement it ends.

Psychoanalysis, as I've indicated, takes a long time because it aims for extensive and lasting change. It also requires a considerable emotional and financial investment. Here the popularity of briefer treatments is easily understandable. At some point you may have thought: "All I need is a change of scenery and I'll get my old enthusiasm back." Or: "I know I'll feel better about myself if I get that new job." Optimism based on situational change is almost universal. So it's not surprising that many people want someone simply to tell them which situational change will remove the problem.

But often, I think, people go beyond this. They accept that the change must come from within. Some may be attracted to modes of treatment that promise rapid change. "If I can once get to my feelings—my real feelings—to let it all hang out, then I'd know my real self. I wouldn't be uptight about sex or about anger." But how does a person "get to real feelings"? For some, the idea of being coached or encouraged to express feelings—to give full vent to emotional outbursts, alone or in groups—is very appealing. Certainly to get rid of something seems simpler than to work to feel it and explore the feelings and thoughts over an extended period of time. In comparison, the work of analysis is laborious; the hope of immediate relief through "venting" cannot be expected.

So, we come back to the question: How can you decide if psychoanalysis is for you? With biofeedback techniques and direct behavioral modification, you might overcome the immediate behavioral limitations of a phobia. With group therapy, you might gain understanding about how you conduct relationships with others. From emotionally expressive therapies or exercises, you might become freer to experience anger or sexual excitement and gain immediate relief. In contrast, what psychoanalysis offers is a chance to find out what is going on inside your mind—to explore thoughts and feelings that may be affecting your life without your knowing it. You will be working actively on your problems with another person, someone who is trained to be empathic and at the same time keep an observer's "distance" so as to offer a clear perspective. As I've explained, psychoanalysis is not easy; deep change never is. Of course you may be hesitant. Everyone is. What's important is that inside you feel that analysis fits your needs and that, with hopeful anticipation, you can commit yourself to at least try. At bottom the question is: "How much do I truly want to work on making lasting changes?" And that's a question only you can answer.

8

Starting Out

"I've done it; I've made a decision: I'm going to begin analysis. It still seems kind of scary. What will it be like? How do I get started?"

THE INITIAL SETTLING-IN

The impact of the first analytic hour varies from analysand to analysand, but it always makes an impression—before, during, and after. Even knowing this, I am sometimes surprised at the changes as I greet a new analysand in the waiting room. Someone who seemed very self-composed during the consultations may be drawn and tense in anticipation of the first hour. In contrast, another person, who previously appeared edgy and irritable, now seems relieved and eager.

The first hurdle is the couch. As I let the new analysand into the office, I observe his or her progress. If the person heads for the couch, I give a look and gesture of encouragement. On the other hand, if the person goes to the chair used during the consultation, I don't interrupt. Perhaps there are some aspects of the arrangements the analysand wants to discuss. If not, I gesture to the couch and say we can begin by his or her lying on the couch and saying what comes to mind. Obviously, if the person is manifestly uncomfortable, I will ask about it. I have found that most analysands require nothing more than simple encouragement and some recognition of their uneasiness. Occasionally someone will feel really "spooked" about using the couch. When this happens, I know the couch has a meaning that will eventually have to be analyzed in depth. To help in the immediate situation, I work with the person to define the problem as much as we each can. What is it that's so disturbing? I indicate the person may remain seated in the chair while gaining familiarity with the basic working principle. But, as soon as possible, when it feels comfortable, he or she should try to use the couch. Rarely has this taken very long.

Every analysand uses the couch in characteristic ways. One person may lie directly in the center, fully in possession of the territory; another may stay timidly at the edge, legs barely on the couch, as if ready to bolt for the door; still another may lie perfectly still, legs crossed, arms across the chest; and yet another may move about, gesturing freely, legs crossing and uncrossing. As I've indicated, the purpose of using the couch is to increase the likelihood of attaining the state of body and mind in which the analysand can best free-associate. Ideally one's body relaxes so that one's physical state is not a focus of attention. Of course body language still participates in communication, but body awareness is reduced and the analysand's attention given over more fully to spontaneous thoughts and feelings.

Lying on the couch frees you of the opportunity or burden (depending on how you look at it) of scanning the listener's face for social regulating responses. The goal is to make it easier to turn your attentiveness inward, to your own thoughts and feelings. But, as I've said before, this isn't easy. You may expect the analyst-listener to have a critical response and avoid reporting a thought that comes to mind. Now you need to ask yourself a question: What lies behind this apprehension? Is it something in the situation or is it coming from inside you? Perhaps you imagine a frown on the analyst's face, or sense a tone of disapproval in the analyst's listening silence. But you can't see the analyst. What is the basis for your conclusions then? Why do you *think* there must be disapproval? The distinction I am trying to get at plays an increasingly significant part in the whole conduct of the analysis, as we shall see.

There are many difficulties in the initial use of the couch. Indeed, sometimes it has the opposite effect from what is intended. Rather than feeling physically relaxed, the new analysand may be tense. It's not quite the same as lying on a beach or on a sofa in the security of one's own den. There's another person there, listening and observing. Again, in some ways, this is reassuring—the sense of a sympathetic listener, not interfering. On the other hand, there may be—and often is—the question: "What is he or she doing? How do I know he or she is on my side?" As in any working relationship, the building of trust between two partners may take time.

Beginnings are invariably awkward. Yet the way out of the initial discomforts is the lead-in for the whole progress of the analysis. The more the analysand focuses on and puts into words the tensions, fears, or sense of strangeness that may accompany the beginning, the more comfortable he or she will feel with the basic working principle. It becomes more familiar. Perhaps a few examples will clarify how the process gets under way and how the analyst facilitates it.

Ms. Allen, after a few moments of hesitation, of not quite knowing where to begin, started to talk about her main complaint. She still wasn't sure what to say and mentioned how strange the couch felt. In a relaxed, nondemanding voice, the analyst asked if she could describe that feeling of strangeness. Encouraged by this remark, Ms. Allen began to reflect on what was making her uneasy. As she did this, she was reminded of other situations that made her similarly uncomfortable. It was a starting point.

After taking a minute to settle himself on the couch, Mr. Karel tried dutifully to follow the basic principle. He noted a crack on the ceiling and commented on the color of the wall. Then he described how his thoughts were flickering and how he was following them. As he chattered on, his voice grew more and more taut and emotionless. The analyst sensed that Mr. Karel was both extremely uncomfortable and so focused on doing what was "expected" that he was probably unaware of his mounting discomfort. At this point the analyst gently noted the signs of Mr. Karel's struggle. When Mr. Karel responded that he did feel uneasy, the analyst encouraged him to verbalize his feelings. With this reassurance, Mr. Karel began the introspective movement from "reporting" his thoughts to talking about them in a much fuller way.

Each of these responses by analysand and analyst moves the analysis forward by setting up a shared relationship between co-workers. The analysand contributes his or her associations. Often those with the most relevance in the beginning are the ones that speak to the struggle with the strangeness and newness of the analytic situation. The analyst in turn contributes his or her attentiveness, listening carefully, inquiring as appropriate, and generally "tuning in." Most relevant to easing the settling-in period may be the analyst's empathic connectedness and sensitive timing about when to share small but, for the analysand, perhaps highly significant insights into what the novice analysand might be experiencing.

BECOMING FAMILIAR WITH THE METHOD

The difficulty of free association comes up repeatedly. Again: to say whatever comes to mind—that's a tall order! Perhaps you are still wondering why it's necessary. Reflecting on this, an analysand might think: "Wouldn't it be better to get to the point about my trouble? But what is the point? I don't really know. After all, that's what I'm in analysis to find out. Maybe the analyst could tell me. But where should I start? What should I talk about? The analyst doesn't answer that question. Couldn't he [or she] at least say where I should start? No, not that either. How can that be right? I don't want to waste this time; I want to talk about what's important. Why can't the analyst tell me?"

The answer is both simple and paradoxical. The analysand is there to explore what is troubling, what is making him or her unhappy, why things aren't working out. But that's part of the problem. The analysand doesn't know why! The nondirective method is designed to enable analysands to convey information that in fact they possess although they don't know they do. One analysand described it as being a middleman. Inside was a fully informed message center that passed its information to him in bits and snatches, like well-disguised pieces of a jigsaw puzzle. Outside was a listener who knew how to penetrate the disguise and put together the pieces of the puzzle into a coherent whole. Yet this description doesn't quite do the analysand's contribution justice. Even the beginning analysand is more than a passive conduit from inside to outside. A better analogy might be to the bard of old who tells his story creatively. He takes the barebone facts and, through his embellishment, gives them meaning, both for himself and for his audience. Adding detail here, tailoring another aspect to his mood, he waxes and wanes with the enthusiasm with which he reveals or hides the significance of his tale. And he never tells the same story the same way twice—the mere fact he has told it before changes its impact for himself and for his listener. Besides, each time he tells it the context he tells it in is different, giving an altered shading to its place in the larger story.

Still, my analysand's description of being a middleman seems accurate for one aspect of the beginning phase. At this point analysands are more reporters of their thoughts and feelings than listeners. They are passing the information along and struggling to accomplish that part of their task. Later in the analysis they will become, more and more, both talkers *and* listeners, reporters *and* interpreters. But at first the listener, and to some degree the interpreter, is the analyst.

This leads to a common question: How does the analyst remember what the analysand says? The beginning analysand tells the analyst a lot of facts about past and present events and concerns, as well as reporting dreams, fantasies, and spontaneous reflections. How can the analyst remember all the events and the whole cast of characters the analysand describes? Moreover, if the nuances and shadings in the telling are significant, how are they remembered? And this for one analysand, let alone for all the patients the analyst is working with. Does the analyst take notes? Tape-record the sessions? Have a phenomenal memory? The answer to these last three questions, in most cases, is "no." Although some analysts may take an occasional note or write down the details of a dream, they usually do not take extensive notes. Only as a part of a research project, and with the analysand's knowledge and consent, would a tape recorder be used. And even if the analyst's memory is above average, it is not phenomenal.

The explanation for analysts' capacity to remember what their analysands say lies elsewhere. They remember because they give a conceptual organization to what they hear. It's not a rote memorizing, but an ordering of information into sequences. Imagine a three-dimensional grid in the analyst's mind. One axis of the grid is based on time—the knowledge of how a boy or a girl matures and develops in each stage of life. Thus, a fact the analysand reveals will be placed into a sequence of development of skills and capacities, outlook, values, and ethics that the analyst is mentally constructing about that particular analysand. A second axis of the grid is based on the expected ups and downs of relationships with significant people at each stage of development. On this axis the analyst organizes information about the "characters" in the analysand's story, listening both to what is said about them and to what is left unsaid. Also on this axis the analyst organizes information about the analytic relationship itself—how the analyst is experienced by the analysand, how the analysand weaves the analyst in and out of the other characters. The third axis of the grid concerns the sequence of the analysis itself. Whatever the analysand relates is considered in terms of the stage of the analysis and what has gone before. Is there a change, for instance, in the depth of introspection? Is the analysand going through a period in which he or she is more reluctant to be self-revealing? And if so, what seemed to trigger this resistance? After months of focusing on problems with competitors, has the analysand begun to shift attention to tender feelings toward some of the same people? And does this change in theme represent an important shift in the analytic work?

All these different "grids" may make the remembering task sound extremely complicated. That perhaps is a limitation of my description. Most analysts, I believe, would state that remembering is not really all that difficult. What *is* difficult is to use one's knowledge of usual patterns while listening to the individual analysand's subjective experience without superimposing preconceptions. Yet it is also true that the more one learns about general human patterns, the more one realizes how unique each individual is.

GETTING OFF THE COUCH

Second to the hurdle of getting on the couch is getting off. Some analysands become so intent on what they are feeling and thinking that they are startled when told the session is over. Occasionally a beginning analysand may jolt upwards, only to feel the dizziness that comes with rising suddenly from a prone position. Many analysands sit on the couch for a moment giving themselves time to catch their breath and adjust to the change.

The initial startle reaction to ending the session and getting up to leave passes in the first week or two. However, reactions to the end of sessions and to separations in general continue throughout the analysis until the final termination. Some analysands develop an inner timeclock that allows them to sense what point they are at in the fifty (or forty-five) minute period. When the analyst indicates that the time is up, they may be able to end the session relatively comfortably. Others do not develop this function until conflicts with endings are worked out and so remain subject to discomfort for a long time. Here the analyst's indication that the session is over may be experienced as a blow—being rejected or pushed out. Still other analysands accurately perceive the time, but are not fully aware of this perception. One man began to falter in his associations about five minutes before the end. He was unaware of this pattern until the analyst noted it for him. Another analysand, a woman, always saved a particularly revealing association until the very end. Again, this unconsciously determined pattern required recognition and eventual analysis. It was as if she were saying: "Please don't make me leave. If I can stay, I'll tell you something you want to hear."

These reactions to the end of the session are similar to everyday responses seen in children and adults. A toddler may beg for one more glass of water before taking a nap, or an adult may want one more drink before leaving a party. At the center are feelings about the dissolution—even temporary—of personal attachments. Mr. Weiss, who became quite distraught at the end of a session, indicated that to keep an inner timeclock as a self-controlling reference point would be too painful. He didn't want to contribute to his "dismissal." Instead, he listened attentively for specific signs from the analyst. Invariably the analyst sat up in his chair a minute or two before the end of the session, and Mr. Weiss could identify the characteristic squeaks. He could tell when the analyst was about to say, "Our time is up," or "We must end now," by the way the analyst cleared his throat and changed his breathing. Mr. Weiss reacted by speeding up his speech. He left no gaps for the analyst to tactfully insert his ending message. The analyst, recognizing this "filibustering," had to break in or let Mr. Weiss remain longer. As Mr. Weiss eventually came to understand, he was saying: "You exercise your control to make a parting; I exercise my control to make a staying."

It's worth noting that in Mr. Weiss' case the understanding of his reactions changed as the analysis progressed. He rejected the idea that the end of the session was a mutually agreed-upon arrangement. At first the emphasis was on his sense that the analyst was pushing him away. Later, it emerged that he wanted to control the ending so that he could push away the analyst.

LEARNING HOW THE MIND WORKS

Defenses

Even beginning analysands expect that if one says one is late because one forgot the time of the hour, the analyst will raise an (unseen) eyebrow. Forgot?—no such thing. That's repression, the motivated removal from awareness of something known. One might imagine an analyst declaring: "You didn't forget because you were busy; you wanted to avoid the analysis. Your problems are becoming more conscious to you. Your lateness reflects your fear of coming; you are trying to protect yourself from what the analysis is revealing." Actually few analysts would use such a confrontative, almost dictatorial approach, and especially not at the beginning. Instead, the analyst may help the analysand focus on the possible meaning by wondering if, looking back on it, the analysand is aware of any feelings that may have played a part in the forgetting.

It is through following the trend of the analysand's associations that the analyst begins to identify the ways in which the person habitually limits the range of his or her self-awareness. Mrs. Warren, for example, began her Monday hour by describing her frustrations when she went to the swim club on Sunday. As the head of the committee on pool safety, she had proposed that no one use the high-diving board unless a lifeguard was on duty. The committee had approved her suggestion by a majority vote. One woman, however, dissented and came over afterward to argue, threatening to demand a ruling by the club's governing board. Mrs. Warren expressed her resentment and indignation at this challenge to her judgment and authority. She then continued with the same theme: she had just begun to relax when her teen-aged daughter came over and asked her for the third time for permission to go to a late movie with her friends. At this point Mrs. Warren's voice changed. Before, in describing her reaction to the committee member, she spoke with heated emotion; now her voice was tired, drained of feeling. She reported that she had explained to her daughter that until school ended, Sunday was a school night and the week-night rules prevailed. In a tone of ineffectualness and defeat, she described how the argument persisted. She mentioned how angry she had been at her daughter, but her voice seemed bland, without feeling.

The analyst recognized the disparity between the way Mrs. Warren spoke of the two challenges, but he also sensed this disparity was not clear to her. Although she was aware of having angry thoughts toward her daughter, unconsciously she had isolated the feelings from the thoughts. The analyst concluded that to be angry at a committee member was acceptable to her but that to feel anger toward her daughter involved some conflict with herself. The basis for that conflict was not yet clear.

Perhaps she feared her anger diminished her image of herself as a good mother in her own eyes or in the eyes of the analyst; or she might fear the intensity of her anger because of unconscious murderous fantasies. Any number of sources of conflict might be hypothesized here. At this point, however, near the beginning of analysis, the analysand needs to learn how the mind works— in this case, how it defends itself against unpleasant thoughts so they stay out of awareness. Thus, the analyst tried to help Mrs. Warren recognize how she automatically separated off her feelings of anger from her thoughts about being angry when she felt threatened by these feelings. Although this defense might temporarily protect her against discomfort, it worked against her in the analysis and ultimately outside as well.

There's a paradox here that may be puzzling. Isn't it sensible and adaptive to protect yourself against discomfort? How can that be working against yourself? Let's return to the analysand who just "forgot" his appointment hour. This person may well believe that he is having trouble enough adjusting to a new and threatening experience. Can't he just leave it that he forgot? After all, he did remember in time; he was only late. He'd feel better about himself thinking that a thought just slipped his mind. Why bring up the possibility that he might be trying to sabotage the very effort he is making at such a sacrifice? It isn't that the analyst doesn't understand this or appreciate the analysand's effort. Indeed, most analysts will point out that such self-protection is a necessary part of adapting, especially when, in growing up, no alternatives seemed available. But the analyst also needs to indicate when the analysand is in opposition to the basic principle. In limiting his time by being late, this analysand is limiting what he can express. Moreover, in his wish that his forgetting be treated as mechanical and unmotivated, he is suggesting that he and the analyst shut off a promising area of inquiry. In the case of analysis, a defense like "forgetting" provides temporary comfort at the expense of an introspective openness to inner awareness.

Eventually, in recognizing the habitual unconscious use of defenses in analysis, the analysand comes to see the limitations of this reduction in self-awareness. For instance, when Mrs.

Warren recognized the disparity in the way she described the two encounters—with the committee woman and with her daughter—she realized that this mirrored her actual behavior in the two situations. She recalled actually speaking to her daughter in a defeated tone, even when her resentment mounted. Without the availability of her angry feelings, her assertiveness suffered, leaving her with a feeling of ineffectiveness and making her relationship with her daughter all the more difficult. Gradually, Mrs. Warren gained insight into the defensive way in which she dealt with her anger toward her daughter. Concurrent with recognition of her defense against anger, she gained greater freedom of expression in the analysis. In time, the conflicts behind this defense became understandable. Consequently, without any particular conscious intentions, she found herself carrying over the freeing up of her emotional expression into her relationship with her daughter—to the relief of both.

With the "forgetting" analysand and Mrs. Warren, I have described in cursory fasion two commonly employed defenses— repression and isolation of affect, to use the "technical" terms. There are fifteen to twenty other, similar means commonly used by *all* people. These defenses give immediate protection from awareness of uncomfortable aspects of one's inner thoughts and feelings, but in the process they diminish the availability of needed internal sources of information. Exploring these ways in which the analysand unconsciously and automatically controls the availability of interpretive information becomes part of the work of recognition and interpretation both early and through the analysis.

Analysands sometimes get the impression that defenses are "bad" and that a goal of analysis is to eliminate them. This view follows the social judgment when, wanting someone to listen to us with an open mind, we say: "You are being defensive; don't be that way." Actually the defense "mechanisms" are simply ordinary ways to regulate thoughts and feelings used unconsciously to protect oneself against information. Freud recognized, for example, that the means by which we protectively isolate the feeling of anger from thoughts, as Mrs. Warren did, is the same way we block out the intrusion of feelings when we need to think clearly to perform, say, a work-related task. It is not the means that is the problem; it is the purpose. Similarly, intellectualizing about a problem to avoid feeling it in depth uses the same mental faculties as intellectual problem-solving. Even when we attribute attitudes and intentions of our own to others because it would give us pain to acknowledge them in ourselves, we employ a means similar to the one that permits us to sense the feelings and thoughts of others. In the analytic work, rather than eliminating defenses (an impossible task), the aim is to recognize their unconscious activity and their purpose. To know why one is unconsciously choosing to isolate one's feelings gives one the possibility to consciously choose to do so or not.

Themes and Patterns

Many people begin their analyses with a theme. Dr. Morris, for instance, regarded his lifelong battle against a conviction of inferiority as the result of his father's neglectful and depreciating attitude toward him. A college professor with a tendency to present his ideas in an orderly, organized manner, Dr. Morris approached the analysis as a situation in which he could gain affirmation for his indictment of his father. At first the analyst did not need to do much more than listen. Occasionally he acknowledged his understanding of the subjective reality Dr. Morris was describing—the painfulness of having an aggressive, nonintellectual, athletic father who disregarded his contemplative, nonathletic interests. His mother had been his refuge, playing word games with him and sheltering him from his father's scathing remarks. Over a period of some months, however, the analyst noted a shift in Dr. Morris's references to the same incidents. Before he had expressed resentment and indignation at his father's callousness. Now he began to express disappointment in their poor relationship. Perhaps if he could have been closer to his father, he would have learned some athletic skills and had an easier time making friends in school. Again, the analyst was not called upon to do more than be attentive and acknowledge the analysand's expanding subjective reality.

Some months later, Dr. Morris pictured his mother in a dream as a jailer keeping a child locked in a pink-colored nursery. His previous ease of speech disapeared; he felt talked out. Even the subject of his father bored him. The analyst recognized a major shift in the pattern of Dr. Morris' approach. His initial theme— the anger he felt toward his father—had been completely self-acceptable. His disappointment in this relationship was a new discovery, one made possible by his feelings of being accepted by the analyst. But the newly emerging theme—the resentment he was beginning to feel toward his mother for her compliance with his avoidance of his father—was not self-acceptable. He felt disloyal to his mother, whom he dearly loved, and he was afraid to lose the sense of her benevolent protectiveness by being critical of her. The result was a complete change in the pattern of the analysis: Dr. Morris became reluctant to talk and for the first time strongly resistant to the analysis as a whole.

Dr. Wasnowski, a clinical psychologist, began her analysis in a very different manner. Priding herself on her memory, she filled most of her hours relating diverse, disconnected anecdotes of the past. Some of these seemed directly related to her major problem, others more remote. She also recounted long, complex dreams and displayed considerable skill in associating to elements in the dreams and giving plausible interpretations of their meanings. During these times the analyst felt as though she were regarded by the analysand as superfluous to the functioning of the analysis. She was relegated to the position of listener and, as she surmised, admirer. Once in a while, however, this pattern was broken, and Dr. Wasnowski would report she felt blue. She yearned to have something good happen, something to cheer her up. The analyst's questions encouraging her to describe her feelings in more detail were now welcomed. Especially she welcomed the analyst's helping her to identify that her sadness was connected with a general feeling of loneliness.

Yet these spells of low spirits were isolated incidents; afterward Dr. Wasnowski would return to her roster of memories and dreams, continuing to brush aside whatever comments the analyst made. The analyst began to notice a significant detail in the pattern of memories and dream self-analyses. Dr. Wasnowski would go on in a particular timeframe—nursery school or adolescence or her unsuccessful first marriage—until she reached a point where someone left. She would relate this as a detail, with no particular feelings, but not long after mentioning it, she would break off the memories of this time period and shift to another. The analyst now appreciated that the timing of Dr. Wasnowski's movement from one timeframe to another was motivated by a defensive need— the need to protect herself from feelings connected with loss. Recognizing this, the analyst was better able to make her interventions in tune with what seemed meaningful to the analysand.

The two examples given are highly individual. Many other themes and patterns in the beginning stages could be described. Each analysand reveals themes and patterns that are characteristic of his or her particular style of relating. Embedded in the "style" are aspects of the individual's conflicts. In the beginning phase, the analyst first tries to become familiar with the analysand's style of relating to the analyst and the analysis. After teasing out the patterns that delineate the person's individual ways of adapting and coping—present and past—the analyst begins the process of aiding the analysand to identify the indicators of vulnerability and conflict in these patterns. At the same time the analyst helps the analysand to note defensive measures that may limit his or her own recognition, as well as methods of disguising communications to the analyst.

Transference

In addition to his remarkable discovery of the unconscious realm of mental life and the special kind of thinking used in dreams and fantasies, Freud pointed to a unique phenomenon called "transference." Transference refers to the way an analysand will, in the analysis, unconsciously repeat a pattern with the analyst—relating to the analyst as if he or she were a figure from the analysand's past. This discovery came as a shock to the dignified Viennese founder of psychoanalysis. At a point when he was encouraging a female patient to reveal memories of her love life, he found that, instead of her remembering the experience in question, she was experiencing erotic desires toward him. The fact that he was a staid physician, older, married, and quite different from her lover, made no difference—the woman's feelings toward Freud were very strong. It is enormously to Freud's credit that he had the courage and scientific discipline to follow through with this discovery of unconsciously repeated feelings and thoughts, learning how to use transference as a consistently present component of psychoanalytic treatment.

To comprehend the phenomenon of transference, let us return to the analyses of Dr. Morris, the college professor, and Dr. Wasnowski, the clinical psychologist. We left Dr. Morris at the point where his mixed feelings about his mother had led to a strong resistance to the treatment. He was no longer invested in criticizing his father yet was still unaware of the dawning criticism of his mother. A new phenomenon appeared in the analysis. In his deprecatory statements about the analysis, he began to assert that the treatment was a trap. It was a way of keeping him dependent. At a time when he should be out competing with other people in the academic world, he was taking shelter in an analyst's office, away from the real world of hard knocks. Sure, the analyst was kind and nice. That only made it worse. Dr. Morris felt he was being seduced into staying close to the analyst by the analyst's thoughtfulness and sensitivity. In listening to these complaints, the analyst began to realize that Dr. Morris had found a remarkable compromise solution for his dilemma. He didn't want to remember how his mother had seductively entrapped him or suffer the guilty feeling of betraying her kindnesses toward him. So he would not "remember" at all. But, then, how could Dr. Morris follow the basic principle, and give expression to the conflict, enabling the analysis to progress? His way out was unconsciously to create a particular image of the analyst. This image was built on the grain of truth in the present: the analyst, like his mother, was kind and the analysis, like his mother's enclosed world of the home, was a haven for him. In this way the analyst and his mother were experienced as the same, with the analyst-mother becoming the source of the feared entrapment from the past.

Again, it is the recognition of a paradox that allows the analysis to move forward. At the same time that Dr. Morris was experiencing the analyst as the mother from his childhood, he also saw the analyst as a professional, as *analyst*. One might draw an analogy to the person at the theater who becomes completely engrossed in a play. A willing suspension of disbelief makes the theater-goer's emotional investment "real" and meaningful. Yet there is always, in the back of the person's mind, an awareness of the play as a play, a fiction. What is different in the analytic situation is that the analysand is not simply a passive spectator, but the inventor of the drama. The balance between the experienced re-creation of the past and the person's current sense of reality takes center-stage. To appreciate the analyst's interpretations of his feelings about entrapment and seduction, Dr. Morris had to recognize the analyst as analyst, as a nonbiased listener to his story. On the other hand, to appreciate how his present behavior toward the analyst was a carry over of a deep concern from the past, Dr. Morris had to *feel* these feelings, to fear the analyst's intentions as he had his mother's. At first, of course, the second half of this clause, the connection to his mother, remained unconscious. But, as Dr. Morris came to recognize this connection, its validity was confirmed by the very experience of transference.

Dr. Wasnowski's initial transference emerged gradually out of the shadows of the themes and patterns of her whole beginning phase. The great sustaining figure of her first ten years had been her maternal grandmother. Her father, a military officer, flitted in and out of her life, as did her mother. Left in her grandmother's home the little girl attempted to be brave and self-sufficient, trying to convince herself she did not miss her parents or the company of other children. Dr. Wasnowski's resentment toward her parents for their desertion was deeply buried. Moreover, her dependence on her grandmother could not be acknowledged without endangering this wall of denial. In the analysis she told anecdotes about her grandmother—but gave no special importance to her. On the other hand, Dr. Wasnowski began to report recent accomplishments to her analyst in a way that seemed to parallel her good reports to her grandmother. She also began to be exquisitely sensitive to the analyst's absences. During the week she managed very well, but over weekends, she felt lonely, blah, and enervated. With longer absences, she felt depressed and fragmented in her functioning. This transference relationship, with the analyst as sustaining grandmother, gradually became clearer, with increased understanding of its origin and meaning.

THE END OF THE BEGINNING

The beginning phase of the analysis is not like the first act of a play. No curtain comes down. Rather, it is like a long introduction to a symphony. Themes are stated, fading in and out in a teasing promise of more to come. Then, in an imperceptible transition, the whole beginning blends into a fuller development, with exposition of a major motif. In analysis, as in music, this point of transition is more easily identified looking back on it than at the time it occurs.

All the analysand's experiences in becoming familiar with the analytic method and in learning about individual defenses and patterns play a part in bringing the beginning phase to a successful close. Yet the feature that most identifies the shift from the beginning to the middle phase is the consolidating, the firming up, of the transference phenomenon. At some point the analysand experiences a feeling of being deeply involved in the treatment. This feeling is not so much a dramatic revelation, more a subtle sensing. One analysand described it this way: "You know, coming here now seems a part of my day—like getting up or going to the office. I do it as a matter of course. And I've gotten to where I think about the analysis the same way. I think about what I'm going to say to you before I come and about what I've said after I leave. I can turn it off of course, but the whole process has become like a part of me."

For some this sense of involvement is reassuring. Others, however, may feel a tinge of anxiety: "I feel like I'm hooked. You occupy a place in my head. I'm talking to you, explaining and arguing. Only in my mind, when I do it, I'm freer. I come here and I start to say what I'm thinking and I don't feel so much like I want to open up. I get all these feelings about you and I'm scared by it. I don't want you to be too important to me. I don't want to get so introspective I'm into myself too much."

In any case, as the middle phase begins, one theme often becomes more consistently the center of focus. With this increased focus, the transference usually takes on a greater intensity. Sometimes the analysand becomes so engrossed in the subjective reality related to this theme that he or she is indeed frightened and may want to run away from the analysis. One man, for instance, was convinced the analyst had the same Calvinist approach to life as his parents. He heard each comment, and even the analyst's silence, as a moral judgment against him for the most trivial indiscretions. What the analyst did was to try to help him maintain an inquiring, exploratory attitude. In this way he and the analyst were able to continue to work within the associative method. Eventually this man began to broaden his awareness of how this childhood conscience was affecting his perception of the present.

Another analysand clung to her reality view of the analyst as therapist as a defense against experiencing transference phenomena. She had heard that all analysands fall in love with their analysts. No such thing was going to happen to her. Yet were erotic feelings, or even affectionate ones, the main transference "danger"? For years this woman had been feared in her family for her quick temper and violent verbal attacks. By rigidly fixing in her mind that her analyst was a doctor who only said things to her as part of his helping function, she was protecting him from her temper and herself from the shame of reacting with inappropriate wrath to a minor slight. With the analyst's help, she was able to recognize this defense and to touch on the fears that lay behind it.

The two analysands just described illustrate two common reactions to the deepening of the analytic exploration—feeling overwhelmed by experiences derived largely from the past or clinging rigidly to the "present" reality of the analytic setup. Most analysands experience some anxiety in the pull toward a more intense involvement in the analytic process. Many have conscious or near-conscious fantasies about stopping. Here the analyst's awareness of the source of the analysand's fears and their indications of progress—of deepening involvement—provides a steadying influence. Through understanding and appropriate interpretation of the various related fantasies, the analyst helps to facilitate the transition from the beginning to the middle phase.

9 Getting Deep into the Middle of the Analysis

"I've been in analysis for a little over a year now. In a way it seems forever, but in another way I feel I've just begun. People tell me I've changed, that I'm more relaxed. It's hard for me to tell. The one thing I know is that the analysis means a lot to me. I'm not sure how it works, but sometimes it's easy for me to say what comes to my mind and I feel good. Other times nothing that means anything to me happens; I feel tied up and unproductive. It looks like a long road ahead. At times I'm tempted to just chuck it. But no, that's not how I really feel. I do want to keep at it, to struggle through, even when it gets tough. It's important. When I feel like I'm associating freely and the analyst points out something and I understand what's going on, I get this sense that my head is clear, that it's all coming together. Then the analysis seems worth all the trouble."

The middle phase of analysis is the period of its major productive work. Yet it is the most difficult to describe. Imagine a painter setting out to do a self-portrait with no preconceived plan, only the goal of creating the most complete and faithful rendition possible. He (or she) might begin with the overall skeletal shape and work on it until a difficulty arose. Then he might shift to the head and face, again persisting until he felt he could proceed no further. Stymied with the main image, he might then work on the background, gradually returning to the figure itself. At this point the artist might change the focus on certain elements—deepening the shadows under the eyes or highlighting the angle of an arm—leading to a completely new approach. As the various areas begin to come together, however, new problems may develop, forcing an extensive reevaluation of the initial conception before work can proceed. It may take a while to work through seemingly contradictory views—to adjust, for instance, the prominence of the cheekbones to the twinkle of a smile. Yet as the discrepancies in perspective are overcome, the momentum of the work picks up. A broadening integration of parts takes hold. All the details begin to "fit." Background and foreground develop a cohesive relation, and the final image achieves a life, a unity, greater than the sum of its parts.

In discussion with colleagues, analysts may use a variety of terms to describe the way the middle phase of analysis unfolds; they may point to the nature of psychic conflict; to regression, resistance, and progression; and to working through. These concepts, however, are generalizations and abstractions—derived from actual experience yet also removed from it. The experience of each analysand is always a unique expression of his or her needs and abilities in interaction with the knowledge and skills of the analyst. It is this that makes the description of psychoanalysis so difficult. The content, the flavor, the "style"— all these are very individual. What I hope to give is some sense of the process through which the "portrait" comes together.

Each session in the analysis might be seen as a microcosm of the total experience. All of the features that can occur in the analysis as a whole can occur in a session. In other words, by looking at what happens in a single session, we can glimpse the overall picture of analysis. At this point you may have a question: Might not one session seem highly productive and another unrewarding? And might not the analysand's and the analyst's view of this differ? In a particular session, the analyst may gain an insight into the nature and source of the analysand's defensive tactics, and so the session seems productive. For the analysand, however, this understanding may not yet be apparent, so the experience may be more one of frustration—unrewarding. Yet what is important to look at here is the process through which understanding comes about. Even if nothing seems to happen, the difficulties are being played out, setting the stage, so to speak, for understanding.

Analysis, then, takes place moment by moment, session by session. Yet, from a different perspective, a description of analytic movement requires the portrayal of change over weeks, months, even years. We can see this in the case of Mr. Hanson, a man in his early thirties. He entered analysis because of concerns about his sexual potency. He felt that before he married, he should rid himself of this worry. During the first year Mr. Hanson talked mostly about the women he dated, describing how his aggressive attitude toward them pushed them away. Toward the end of the beginning phase, he formed a defiant transference reaction toward the analyst. One day he came in and stated he had not remembered any dreams—and he was glad of it. He didn't feel like going along with the analyst's wishes anymore. He felt like marrying any woman who would have him and quitting the analysis. Who said he had to work out his problems about manliness before getting married? Throughout the whole week Mr. Hanson's attitude remained much the same. He had thoughts he'd rather not talk about. Not because they were secret or special; just because he didn't want to be a good patient who did what he was told. He was, so to speak, on strike. At one point he "slipped" in his resolve, mentioning that when he had worked in his father's store he had felt similarly. Immediately, however, he caught himself: that was "associating" and that was what he refused to do.

This defiant attitude toward the analyst, with its hint of a transference from his father, heralded the start of the middle phase. It also signaled the theme for the first fifteen months of the main working phase: Mr. Hanson's relations to authority figures. Over a period of months, he moved from an attitude of defiance to one of compliance and passive resignation. Then came a period of depression, marked by a bemoaning of his fate and a feeling of weakness. From this, Mr. Hanson drifted into bodily complaints. If he drank too much, he feared his liver would be permanently damaged, as his father had warned. In his dreams, large, frightening men threatened him with physical harm of one sort or another. Now Mr. Hanson turned to idealizing the analyst. He wished he could be as steady and self-reliant as the analyst seemed. It was such a contrast to his father. How could he feel like a man with such a father?

Gradually Mr. Hanson's perspective shifted. The analyst helped him see that, along with his idealizing, he also pictured the analyst, in only lightly disguised forms, as treating him as he complained his father had. Mr. Hanson came to acknowledge that it suited some of his wishes to belittle the contributions of both his father and the analyst. As long as he remained the "little boy" when the big men threatened but didn't help, he could wait for the analyst to produce a change in him and avoid the risk of failing or being rejected. With this recognition of his commitment to passive avoidance, and with the belief that it lay within his choice to change and be more active, Mr. Hanson's spirits lifted. At the end of this fifteen-month period he began to show a renewed interest in dating, with a new confidence. The next phase of the analysis then centered on his relationship with his mother and his two sisters.

This synopsis gives only a hint of the complexity of analytic change. I have highlighted the shifts in themes, yet each theme returned from time to time and had to be reexamined. Underlying the waxing and waning of themes is the activity of the analyst and analysand in understanding how the analysand creates and perceives his or her experiences. Here we need to examine how the analysand's contradictory wishes, attitudes, and values color the actions and subjective reality the analysis brings to light.

WHAT DO PSYCHOANALYTIC CONCEPTS TELL US?

Psychic Conflict

"Psychic conflict" is a term that has been defined in many different ways as psychoanalytic thinking about mental functioning has changed. What does it mean in terms of the "everyday life" of analysis? Let us look again at Mr. Hanson and his relations to authority figures. Listening to him, the analyst was struck by the number of conflicts he had with people over issues of authority: Mr. Hanson was provocative with his immediate supervisor, cowed by and unduly compliant with service station attendants, belligerently assertive with his young nephew. He had trouble not only when others were in positions of authority but also when he himself was. This type of conflict is called *interpersonal* conflict, and psychoanalysis draws on it for data to make inferences about the type of conflict analysts primarily focus on—*intrapsychic* conflict. Intrapsychic conflict refers to a situation in which opposing tendencies exist within the person's modes of thinking, feeling, and acting. Mr. Hanson, for instance, showed conflicting tendencies in his alternatively defiant and compliant, depreciating and idealizing behavior.

Wait, you may object, he was defiant and compliant toward the *analyst*—isn't that interpersonal? The answer is "yes" and "no." Yes, the manifestations of this conflict occurred in an interpersonal context, between the analysand and the analyst. But no, the origin was not truly interpersonal; it was intrapsychically determined by the analysand. How can I make such a startling claim? The explanation lies in the nature of transference. Mr. Hanson "used" the analyst as the person toward whom he expressed his opposing tendencies. First he was defiant, then compliant, bringing out the conflictual nature of these intrapsychic attitudes over time. On the other hand, with regard to the opposing tendencies of depreciation and idealization, he expressed both at once, feeling one toward his father and the other toward the analyst.

Wait again, you may exclaim: Wasn't his behavior simply a reaction to the interpersonal situation? As before, "yes" and "no." From one view, the analyst was an authority who gave him a "rule" of free association to follow and his defiance and compliance were in response to that. But how accurate is that picture? Was the analyst truly an authority pushing the analysand to do his bidding? The "rule," after all, was a working principle Mr. Hanson had accepted and agreed to. Nor did the analyst react to Mr. Hanson's defiance with threats, in this way producing the compliance. Throughout the shifts in Mr. Hanson's behavior, the analyst offered the same attentive, generally quiet, supportive interest. As an interpersonal response, Mr. Hanson's reaction was a mountain of emotion stirred up by a molehill of truth. Moreover, he "knew" that there was a discrepancy between the actual situation and the intensity of his response. One might say that the analysand uses the "little" truths of actual interpersonal situations that analysis provides to express feelings and thoughts that fit in with deep-seated preconceptions and expectations. When the person's habitual modes of thinking, feeling, and acting are based on opposing tendencies, each side gains ascendancy in the analysand's associations at some point or another in the analysis.

All right, you might say, being defiant at one time and compliant at another to the same request of the analyst *is* a contradiction. It doesn't fit the immediate situation so some other factor must be at work. It might even be that as a little boy, Mr. Hanson reacted this way to one or both of his parents. But what about his depreciating and idealizing? Isn't it true that the analyst had helped him? He was feeling better and going out with women. And hadn't his father failed him? Didn't he give convincing illustrations of this? Why do you call that evidence of intrapsychic conflict?

Here I need to add a few more details from Mr. Hanson's analysis. During the period in which he was depressed, bemoaning his fate, the analyst observed that anything Mr. Hanson accomplished inside or outside the analysis, he pooh-poohed. For weeks, for instance, he talked about the importance of a task he was working on. Yet when he successfully completed it, he minimized and depreciated his achievement. The analyst noted this shift. Mr. Hanson responded: "It's easy for you to talk. You've got it made. A wife, a big house, whatever you want. You probably slept with all the girls you wanted when you were in college instead of having them run away from you like they did from me." The angry envy expressed here may be startling, given the mildness of the analyst's comment. The analyst has everything (the idealized picture); the analysand nothing (the depreciatory view) in an all good/all bad extreme. In a similar way, the memories of his father Mr. Hanson brought up at this time all reinforced the picture of a father who had contributed *nothing* to his manhood. Yet these memories seemed to represent an unconsciously selected biased sampling. Details from his associations about the analyst's ideal qualities suggested that this view was transferred from attitudes he had once held toward his father.

In attempting to understand the analysand's problems, the analyst does not seek to reconstruct past events or relationships as they might exist in a photographic record. First, it would not be possible; memory is too selective. Second, the meaning of a particular occurrence is not "set." Events and relationships in one phase influence subsequent development, but later phases also reorganize the import of what has gone before. Third, it is not necessary to remember exactly what happened. The analyst and analysand need only to understand the meaning of events in the analysand's subjective experience for the analysand to make use of the insight. By understanding the meaning present and past experiences have for how one feels and thinks, one gains the insight necessary to make a conscious choice where previously one might have reacted inflexibly, based on unconscious "memories."

All this may be confusing, so I'll attempt a further clarification. An adult's intrapsychic conflicts reflect opposing tendencies that originate both in the person's inborn proclivities and in a whole past history of individual experiences with people and things. Even from the earliest moments of life, it's hard to distinguish between these two influences—inborn inclinations and life experiences. Each impacts on the other to such a degree that their effects become intertwined in the developing child's personality structure. Let's take Mr. Hanson as an example again. What if, as a toddler, he were simply "normally" defiant (as children of about two years tend to be), but his mother "overreacted," expressing considerable distress and anger at his little-boy expressions of "will"? He might have had difficulty in tempering this "natural" tendency and been forced to bury it under compliance as a way to hold his mother's love and approval. On the other hand, what if he had an inborn tendency to be strongly negativistic, as may happen with some children?

Perhaps his mother, although usually a patient woman, was strained beyond her limits. She might then have urged compliance as a relief from the strain—accepting a pseudo-solution to the problem. In either case, then, the reaction to authority would retain a conflictual element, alternating between defiance and compliance.

Is that the end of the story? No. As I said before, later development may alter the picture (or reinforce it). In Mr. Hanson's case, with the greater capacities for order of a three-to-four-year-old, he was better able to comply with his mother's expectations. Their relationship took a dramatic turn for the better, augmented by the erotic love that generally blossoms between the little boy and his mother at this time. On the other hand, the tension between father and son that tends to flare up at this time provided a new battleground for the unresolved conflict with authority. What happened when the father attempted to discipline his son; how did the father react to his son's compliance or rebellion? Obviously one factor here was the father's actual behavior. Yet the boy's experience of the father's reaction was also colored by what had happened earlier, with his mother, around discipline. Even more, boys at this age have various fantasies about their rivalry with the father as the mother's lover. If, as a little boy, Mr. Hanson imagined that his father saw him as a dangerous competitor, he might read the father's disciplinary action as a confirmation of this fantasy. In other words, his concept of his manliness might become attached to the whole issue of defiance or compliance. And then, again, later encounters would add or take away from this perception. My point is that the conflicts the analysand brings into analysis are determined by many, many factors. There is no one memory that tells it all.

Another aspect of unresolved intrapsychic conflicts is their persistence and repetition. This explains not only why the analysis of them is necessary, but, in a sense, what makes it possible. Unresolved conflicts push the analysand into unconsciously perceiving and reacting to the analyst in accordance with the subjective slant set up by the opposing tendencies. In other words, in the analysis, the analysand is compelled to repeat the expression of these conflicting tendencies. One might say the person is compelled to be him- or herself, however much the person may try to mask the conflicts or explain their expression away as only reactive to a particular situation. At first an analysand like Mr. Hanson may believe that he is only reacting to the analyst, that the analyst is "causing" his defiance or compliance. As he explores his experience more, he may come to recognize the discrepancy between the intensity of his response and the relative insignificance of the stimulus the analyst provides. But this recognition is never simple. The pattern being repeated is usually one that has taken hold through a variety of experiences, with a multifaceted history. I've suggested how Mr. Hanson's encounters first with his mother and later with his father affected the conflict between defiance and compliance. During grade school his defiance was almost completely buried. As he described it, he was seen as an agreeable and cooperative student, although perhaps a bit lacking in assertiveness. In early adolescence he continued for the most part to be compliant in school but began to react defiantly at home to minor restrictions and requests that he keep his room in order. Then, in later adolescence, he became unexpectedly argumentative and belligerent with certain teachers, although with other teachers, whom he idealized, he was quite cooperative, a follower and a champion of their ideas. At this time his defiance toward certain school rules kept him on the edge of serious disciplinary action, an edge he never quite fell over.

Recall my analogy to the artist painting a self-portrait. The painter began at some point but, after some success, became stalled and started again in another area. Each effort, even if temporarily abandoned, gave him a slightly altered perspective. So it is with vistas on conflicts. In the analysis Mr. Hanson's defiance might feel like his adolescent rebellion against teachers or his struggle at age four or five with his father, or like the earlier battle with his mother. It is such shadings derived from the past that color the present—sometimes grossly (as in Mr. Hanson's interaction with his boss) but often more subtly, particularly in the analysis, where these tensions are simultaneously "happening" and being explored. Looking at them changes them too, giving the experience a sense of being controlled and controllable.

I have indicated two reasons why the concept of psychic conflict is central to an understanding of how psychoanalysis works. First, it explains what the analyst and the analysand are working to resolve. Second, it explains in part what propels the analytic movement, for the person keeps trying to find a resolution to the opposing pulls. Faulty efforts from the past are repeated, but in a context that provides a chance for new understanding. There is yet a third reason for the importance of the concept of psychic conflict: it explains a crucial aspect of what permits the analyst to serve as an empathically sensitive listener. The analyst is someone who is open to the intrapsychic conflicts, the opposing tendencies, in his or her own makeup. The old adage applies: it takes one to know one. Only we must add: it takes a specially trained one to treat one. Psychoanalytic training requires that the analyst go through an extensive analysis as an analaysand with another analyst. In this way the analyst has confronted his or her own unresolved conflicts as a patient and, it is hoped, come to resolve them. Yet part of the task of being an analyst is to retain an introspective connectedness to one's internal struggles. One might look at it this way: most analysands wish to integrate their opposing tendencies as much as possible, in order to get on with their lives more effectively. For the analyst, effective getting on with life as an analyst involves both integrating opposing tendencies as much as possible *and* remaining in touch with them.

You may wish to raise an objection: What if the analyst's conflicts are different from the analysand's? In truth, the analyst's conflicts have to be different—each person's conflicts are as individual as his or her fingerprints. But, on a general level, each person must confront similar pulls—toward activeness or passiveness, lovingness or anger, getting immediate pleasure or satisfying one's conscience, and so on. These polar inclinations arise in response to the experiences of nursing, learning to control one's bodily functions and to regulate sexual excitement, moving (literally and symbolically) away from one's parents, handling argument and controversy, and all the many other common aspects of growing up.

All right, you may say—as many of my analysands have—in the broad outlines people go through similar phases in life, which present similar difficulties. But how far can empathy for another's experiences stretch? Can, for example, a male analyst know how a woman feels? How can he know what it feels like to have a baby? Or to grow up with a vagina? Alternatively, how can a female analyst know what a little boy feels about his penis? Isn't there a danger that the analyst will simply superimpose a theory? What if a male analyst sees a woman's conflict in terms of penis envy when her anger is over the male's privileged position in the family? My answer is that with any analyst, male or female, working with any analysand, male or female, there is always a danger of a failure of empathy—momentary or prolonged. But I don't believe the problem behind such lapses in empathic contact is the lack of a similar experience on the analyst's part. Instead, what may happen is that the analyst's own unresolved conflicts lead him or her to defend against the introspective self-awareness needed for empathic listening. In this instance the analyst is in the same position as the analysand, struggling to keep the conflict out of awareness. In other words, the analyst's past experience interferes with an unbiased responsiveness to the analysand's associations.

Obviously this should happen as little as humanly possible. It is one reason why it is so important for analysts to have had a thorough analysis of their own. Moreover, analysts are trained to perform an ongoing self-analysis, to monitor their own reactions with an eye to the recrudescence of conflicts and the need for their further analysis. Unfortunately, no system is perfect, but in general a well-trained analyst will not remain embroiled in unresolved conflicts that impair empathy. Thus, it should be possible for a male analyst to understand a female analysand and vice versa.

It is generally assumed that a male portrait painter can sensitively portray a woman and a female novelist give a convincing character study of a man. The creative artist is uniquely open to the nuances of feeling in a broad spectrum of other people, which he or she conveys through the art form. The analyst is like the creative artist in this openness. In the analyst this openness is commonly enhanced by persisting identifications with parents and others of both gender. Male analysts, for instance, have often been very close to their mothers and have developed a maternal caretaking sensitivity. Similarly, female analysts have often sensed deeply into the male world. For the analyst, then, the ability to listen, without superimposing a theoretical bias comes from an empathic openness, as well as from extensive training. Earlier I mentioned how the analyst organizes the information in the analysand's associations. At the same time that this organization structures a portrait of the analysand, it remains fluid, open to change; it is not prematurely closed.

Regression, Resistance, and Progression

Picture a man lying on a beach. No one is near and the weather is perfect, sunny and warm. His mind drifts from thought to thought. He thinks of his job and the promotion he hopes to get. He pictures himself telling Jane about it. She is pleased. They go out for a lovely dinner and come back to his place. He is very smooth in his sexual approach and they have intercourse; it's beautiful. Just thinking about it, he gets aroused. Then a thought intrudes: she'll start up about marriage again. Someday he has to face this issue with her, but he doesn't feel ready yet. He remembers when he was so eager to marry he couldn't stand it; he was so in love with Betty. But his father said he was too young, he was still in college, and threatened to cut off all his support. His mother became hysterical. He capitulated. It was probably for the best, but he's never gotten over it . . . and Paul's death in the car crash. His best friend. How he misses him. It's like when his uncle George died. Uncle George was so helpful when he was a child, when he was so scared of things. But what is he doing thinking about death on such a beautiful day? It's morbid. He should be thinking about something good—

something happy. Like his younger brother's upcoming visit. They'll have a good time, go to see the Orioles; it'll be like old times.

Or imagine a woman sitting in a chair, gently rocking her dozing baby. Her mind plays over the recent past. How happy she's been since the baby was born. It makes all the trouble she had getting pregnant worth it. And things are better now with Harry. It was awful before; they were so tense. They couldn't stop blaming each other. He kept saying she was castrating him. She denied it, but it's always worried her. Did she? Her career went better than his for a while; she knew that got to him. Like when she was better in school than her brother Jim. Her mother couldn't stand it. She accused her of lording it over him. Will her mother come and visit her now that she has the baby? She goes to Jim's all the time. That hurts. It always has. Oh well, she should be used to it now. Will the baby be pretty? She hopes so—she was. It was fun—being looked at by the boys.

These are examples of the thinking and feeling that takes place in a state of regression. Although they resemble the free association of the analysand in psychoanalysis, they differ in that they are not simultaneously an attempt to communicate with an analyst to achieve a therapeutic goal. They are simply common, everyday experiences. You yourself may have had similar thoughts. And this may help you to appreciate what is meant by a "regressive" state of mind. It has its rules, its sequences, its inner plan. It moves toward the wish-fulfilling pleasures of a daydream, but it includes troubling elements that temper these wish fulfillments. It moves back and forth between present and past, linking one element to another not so much by logic of time and place but by emotional sequence. Most of all, it allows one to say a lot about oneself, coming as close to honesty as one can get. It's not really goal-oriented, like a work task. It's more to keep oneself company, to "talk" to oneself about one's thoughts and feelings. Still, some stocktaking occurs, some planning for the future, some learning from the past.

All too often people think of regression as something babyish, backward, meaningless. In extreme cases, of course, regression may lead to childlike behavior, but it is rarely meaningless.

Indeed, in the form I've just described it is of incontestable value. The whole framework of analysis is designed to encourage this type of regressive state of mind in the analysand. There are two reasons for this. First, the thoughts and feelings expressed in the regressive state of mind are highly informative about the individual. From the two examples I've given, you may have a beginning sense of acquaintanceship with each person. The man on the beach, for instance, reveals something of his problems with decision-making as well as his lingering sadness over the loss of important people in his life. The woman expresses her competitiveness, as well as her sense of achievement. We get hints from each about significant past relationships. And all from a few moments of commonplace reflection in the regressive state of mind!

The second reason that this mode of thinking is encouraged in analysis is that it enhances the likelihood that transference phenomena will occur. Remember the distinction between everyday regressive reflections and psychoanalytic free association—that in analysis there is a listener to whom the thoughts and feelings are communicated. When reflections from the regressive state of mind are expressed to an analyst, the conscious and unconscious wishes and attitudes contained within them tend to become focused on the analyst. If the musings of the man on the beach and the woman rocking her baby were spoken aloud to an analyst in the middle phase of analysis, the whole context would be different. The analyst would have a considerable background of information from which to draw inferences about the meaning of these "associations." For the sake of illustration, however, let's imaginatively place them in an analytic context. Then we could ask: What hidden references to the analyst might they contain? Assume that the man is beginning to become aware of how much he desires the analyst's approval. His mention of his manly wooing of Jane might be in hopes of impressing the analyst. If the analyst were to remain silent, he might take the absence of affirmation as an indication that his analyst morally disapproves. Rather than deal directly with this touchy matter of his disappointment and fear, he associates to the past—to his parents' disapproval of his relation to Betty. It might then be that an underlying feeling of estrangement from the analyst (seen as disapproving) stimulates the thoughts about the death of two supportive figures, his best friend and his uncle George. Finally his wish for the analyst to join him breaks through in his "association" to his brother's upcoming visit.

With the woman, let's imagine that competition has figured as a central theme in the analysis. She begins by inviting the analyst to share in her pleasure in her baby. Perhaps a residue of resentment toward the analyst begins to surface before the analyst even has a chance to note her wish. Her repeated fear of being criticized unjustly takes hold and her mood changes. Her concern about being castrating might then be an unconscious reference to the analyst-listener. Is the analyst, like her husband and her mother, one who finds her too competitive? Is the analyst's silence as she recalls the past pains of unjust accusations an assent to the same criticism? When she wonders if her mother will come to her house to see the baby, might she be asking why the analyst doesn't "come to visit," that is, speak to her? Is it because he (or she) prefers his male analysands? Well, at least she's pretty! She can take comfort in that!

Obviously all this is highly conjectural, for in analysis the sequence of the associations would, at every point, be affected by the analyst's presence as listener. Were the man's reflections expressed in analysis, he might not think of Jane as the one raising the question about his indecision about marriage, but the analyst. He might then choose to focus on the feeling of being involved in a struggle with the analyst about his decision. Everything that followed might then be different. Caught up in the struggle with the analyst, the man might not go on to his romance in college and the deaths of his best friend and uncle. But what if these connections are important, revealing? Is the focus on the analyst a sign of resistance?

The situation may seem paradoxical—a kind of catch-22. If, as an analysand, one expresses the wishes and attitudes that arise in the regressive state of mind toward the analyst, one may in effect be resisting recognition of the source of these wishes and attitudes within oneself and one's past experiences. On the other hand, if one expresses the relation of these wishes and attitudes to figures in one's present and past life, one may in effect be resisting recognition of the importance attached to the analyst's response. Does this mean that whatever analysands say, they are resisting? Isn't the opposite also true—that whatever analysands say, they are expressing their feelings and thoughts, communicating information about themselves? The answer lies in between, in the degree of freedom, of flexibility, the analysand experiences in moving back and forth between present and past, between outside figures, self, and analyst, depending on which bears the predominant weight of his or her feelings. When a male analysand is primarily concerned about the analyst's disapproval of his sexual activities, is he free to address that concern? Or is the discomfort of guilt or the fear of prohibiting interference from the analyst so great that he unconsciously avoids this by shifting his concerns elsewhere? If the analyst then suggests to this man that he *is* concerned with the analyst's reaction, is he free to consider this interpretation and appraise its validity? Or does he react negatively to the interpretation, decidedly avoiding any consideration of the analyst as the possible focus for his feelings? Does he then find it increasingly difficult over a period of time to get any real understanding or sense of clarity about his state of mind? It is when the latter happens that one speaks of the analysand being in a state of resistance.

But now what? you may ask. Does the analysand just remain in this state of resistance? Usually, over time, there is a change in the person's motivations and an increased willingness to look at the source of resistance. The very recognition that something is blocking progress in the analysis may enable the analysand to free up his or her associations again and explore what the resistance is in reaction to.

How, then, can psychoanalytic progression be conceptualized? Is it the opposite of analytic regression and resistance? No—quite the contrary! Analytic progression depends on the analysand's ability to establish a regressive state of mind and to experience transference phenomena toward the analyst. Because transference responses are deeply felt in the present interaction with the analyst and at the same time are linked to past experiences, they provide a fertile avenue for exploring just how past perceptions may be coloring and distorting the present. Moreover, analytic progress continues even if, in response to an interpretation or to ward one off, the analysand unconcsciously resorts to a state of resistance. Just by instituting a state of resistance, the analysand underlines the significance of a particular conflict. The nature of the resistance—its form and content—gives invaluable clues to its purpose. The analytic work proceeeds through the interpretation of the resistance and the unresolved opposing tendencies that underlie it. In the middle phase, then, the analysis moves forward as the analysand experiences increasing ease in establishing the regressive state of mind. Transferences and resistances emerge more freely, are interpreted and understood more readily, and new versions of the conflicts appear for working through.

Working Through

An analysand of mine, familiar with the theories and terminology of psychoanalysis, defined "working through" as a damnable process whereby the analysand has to keep reinventing the wheel. What my analysand was referring to was her experience of bringing up an area of conflict, gaining insight into it, feeling she had mastery over it, only to reexperience similar struggles in slightly altered versions over and over again. Naturally this was frustrating to her—and disappointing. But it is this very process of repeated reworking of areas of conflict that constitutes the principal means by which psychoanalysis, unlike briefer psychotherapies, accomplishes major changes in painful, ineffective ways of experiencing and reacting that seem part of the very fabric of the self. My analysand used her knowledge to give herself consolation: she reasoned that it had taken her twenty-four years to get to be the person she was when she began her analysis; it would take considerable time to learn about and undo the parts she needed to change.

But why should one have to go over the same problems and conflicts again and again? After all, if you work out the proof of a mathematical theorem, for instance, you come to understand it. You have a "hold" on it and can go on from there, without having to prove it again. My analysand, whose grasp of abstract intellectual concepts was of a very high order, could not accept that her grasp of the meaning behind a transference issue was not retained in the same way. Yet there is an essential difference between achieving insight into an abstract problem, like a mathematical theorem, and understanding one's own behavior. The mathematician wishes to retain the information and build on it—it enhances him or her in all respects. Of course my analysand also wished to retain and enjoy the benefit of her insight. The information, however, was associated with a great deal of anxiety, depression, and embarrassment. Did she really want to stir up all this psychic pain? In other words, she also had a powerful motive to "forget" any insight she gained. It is the unconscious instituting and reinstituting of resistance that necessitates the bit by bit working through of problem areas in psychoanalysis.

Complex as this sounds, it is only one of the reasons why a lengthy period of working through is required. Another reason concerns the way memory works. Unlike a tape recorder, which retains an unselective record, playing back not only the spoken voice but also often the street noises in the background, the human memory actively screens both what is retained and what is recalled. There is a lot we still do not know about this process, for the "coding" of memories, how they are stored, is quite complex. On the whole, however, it can be said that we tend to retain the significant rather than the trivial—which gives memory a greater objective fidelity than that of the undiscriminating tape recorder. Yet we are more likely to consciously recall the more emotionally acceptable than the more troubling—which contributes to a subjective rather than an objective rendition. In some instances, then, a trivial detail may be recalled because it is emotionally bland while a disturbing significant event is "forgotten." In other instances the lesser of a series of disturbing events or relationships will be recalled, serving as a screen against the others. Thus, although the memories the analysand reports usually indicate the importance of an event, often they appear in a disguised and distorted, partial form that obscures the troubling side of the "record."

In the first stage of analysis with a male analyst, Ms. Kelly reported a memory of her father making a sarcastic remark about her. She felt hurt by him and close to her mother as a co-victim of masculine arrogance. This feeling of being victimized by men played an important part in her transference reaction to the analyst and required considerable working through, as she brought forth a series of memories of her suffering from repeated depreciating comments by her father and other men. She frequently construed the analyst's comments as similarly belittling.

Later, in the middle phase of the analysis, when the same memory of her father's derogatory comment came up, it had another meaning. Then it seemed to serve as a screen for another hurt—a deep one. She believed that her mother had been deeply disappointed in her because of a birth defect (which had later been corrected by surgery). For full understanding, it was necessary for Ms. Kelly to repeatedly bring up this memory and the feelings of hurt and deflation that were a part of it. These repetitions made it possible to explore, first, the significance of the memory as a source of information about her relationships with men and, second, its significance as a screen. The closeness of mother and daughter in the first reported memory of the father's sarcastic remark covered up a painful sense of estrangement related to her birth defect, which was even more deeply troubling.

But this same memory was still to reveal another "secret," successfully screened by selective recall. Her father's sarcastic remark itself had been recalled with many details. What was left out, until late in the middle phase, was what had preceded it. The little girl and her father had been enjoying a moment of tender intimacy when the mother entered. It was then that the father had made the sarcastic remark. The initial memory, then, focused on the tension between father and daughter, obscuring their closeness and the shutting out of mother that the little girl felt guilty about. What Ms. Kelly remembered was not the guilt-producing intimacy, but the guilt-assuaging put-down by her father. I hope this example gives a glimmer of the necessity to go over and over the details of associations in order to understand the multiple meanings that memories simultaneously include and disguise.

Still another reason exists for the need to repeatedly consider and interpret similar reactions. In its reexamination of past and present experiences, analysis involves a shifting between childhood and adult perceptions. It is characteristic of the regressive state of mind that the analysand's perspective on responsibility is similar to that of the child. Children, for instance, often have difficulty distinguishing between fantasy and action. They may, for instance, in a state of hurt anger, wish mother were dead and even voice this in play: "Bang! Bang! You're dead!" They may then feel guilty, far out of proportion to any possible effect, clinging to mother to make sure she isn't really hurt. When the feelings toward a parent are strongly ambivalent, and if the parent actually becomes ill or suffers a mishap, the child may experience an excessive guilt reaction, as if he or she were responsible. On the other hand, children distort their parents' part. A little boy who becomes carsick on a trip, for example, is apt to blame his parents for his plight.

Children, especially young children, are in fact highly dependent on their parents for both the emotional and the physical regulation of their daily lives. The parents' caring brings deep attachment and joy, but regulatory failures cause pain and, if frequent, may be experienced as grievous deficiencies in empathy. My purpose in saying this is to point out that our experience is an individually created amalgam of actual events and relationships and our abilities and limitations at different ages to construe these happenings. Whatever the parents' "mistakes"— and no parent is perfect—the analysand's task is to free the experiencing of the present from distorted perceptions based on the past. Yet the analysand must reexamine the childhood perceptions in a regressive state of mind for them to have emotional validity. Only after many previously unconscious aspects of the painful experience have been brought into awareness is the analysand in a position to reconfront the experience from an adult perspective. Because the emotional pull of unconscious assignments of responsibility, whether to the self or to others, is very strong, this process of examining the assignment of blame and responsibility to oneself and to others must be worked through over an extended period of time.

A final reason for the length of time working through takes is the need for the analysand to shift from a relatively passive to a relatively active orientation toward the analytic work. In the beginning the analysand's orientation tends to be passive—the one who is done to. For many, the past is experienced as what has happened to them. Their inexplicable guilt or anxiety feelings, as well as their symptoms, are like foreign bodies grafted onto them. The analytic work of interpreting is something the analyst does to and for them. Insight is to be provided. Admittedly, I have exaggerated this passive tendency, but it does exist as a general expectation. As a consequence, many analysands tend to experience others as the cause of their difficulties or the source of their rescue. As the analysis proceeds, however, they become more active in contributing to the interpretive work of the analysis. They themselves begin to sense when they might be defending against a perception. And they can more actively confront one perspective on their experience and respond with other perspectives. Thus, the same conflicts must be viewed and re-viewed as the analysand's perspective shifts from passive to active for the conflicts to be fully and effectively worked through, and termination considered.

10 Endings and New Beginnings

"I've thought several times now about ending my analysis. At first it seemed just a defense against working, or maybe wishful thinking. But I'm not sure—there's something positive in it, more like moving out of my own than running away. And I keep thinking about it at odd moments. I've learned that when I keep thinking about something I should take my thoughts seriously and bring it up in analysis. But what will Dr. Jones say? Maybe he'll laugh: 'That's ridiculous!' Or maybe he'll congratulate me: 'That's great!' Now I am being silly. He'll probably say his usual: 'We'll have to analyze that.' Still, I'm going to bring it up."

RECOGNIZING THE BEGINNING OF THE END

Children in kindergarten know that when summer comes school will come to an end. College students know that on completing their senior year and earning all their credits, they'll get a degree. Clearly delineated time periods and accomplishments define the progression and the end-point. Not so with psychoanalysis. The time it takes is highly variable, and there are no easy-to-define accomplishments like passing courses.

Nor is recovery from illness a useful analogy. The treatment of an infection ends when the fever comes down, the malaise disappears and the physician judges the danger of recurrence over. Or the rehabilitation of a knee after surgery may end when an optimal return of functioning has been achieved. For the analysand, however, no thermometer registers the end of a fever. Nor is there any specific standard—such as the arc of movement of a normal knee—to measure optimal functioning. Yet, on the basis of introspection, the analysand often has a reasonably reliable sense of the possibility of the beginning of the end.

Sometimes analysands make their estimate on the basis of a symptom change that affects their lives outside of the analysis. A man with a travel phobia may feel he can now move about without limiting restriction. Or a woman who suffered from periods of depressive withdrawal alternating with compulsive sociability may regard herself as freer to choose when she really wants companionship. At other times the opinion may come from a symptomlike change within the analysis. An analysand who originally complained of depression, irritability, and boredom may have already experienced a marked diminution of these painful feelings in his general living but remained troubled by how these emotions kept recurring periodicaly within the analysis. His consideration of an ending date may stem from a belief that he has come to understand the meaning of these symptoms as they appear in his responses to the analyst. Often analysands contemplate ending after weathering a vacation from the analysis in a way they believe indicates their readiness to "be on their own."

Whatever the specific spur to the thought of ending, the idea creates its own tensions for the analysand. A frequent fear is that the thought of ending may be motivated by an unconscious desire to avoid some conflict. This possibility is especially troubling for analysands who have regularly entertained fantasies of quitting when they were resisting. And even if the analysand is satisfied that this time the idea is based on progress in the analysis, there's still the fear that the analyst will disagree. This fear has two sides. What if the analyst proves to be correct in disagreeing and the idea of ending is in the interest of resistance? It might be embarrassing, a blow to the analysand's confidence. On the other hand, what if the analyst fails to recognize the appropriateness of the analysand's suggestion and incorrectly disagrees? It might weaken the analysand's confidence in the analyst's empathy and judgment.

Not all the analysand's concerns center on the analyst's rejecting the suggestion that termination (as analysts call it) should be considered. A "yes" answer also carries fears. Perhaps the analyst will agree to the idea of ending, but some important problem will be left overlooked. Or an analysand may believe himself to have been a "difficult patient: Does the analyst just want to get rid of him at the earliest opportunity? An analysand who had this fear described it as the analyst's taking Senator Aikin's advice for ending the Vietnam War: Declare it a victory and leave. A common fear of analysands concerns being left without the supportive aspects of analysis.

Despite these fears, the conviction that one is ready to consider termination may persist. The analysand may believe that important conflicts have been worked out sufficiently to see the "light at the end of the tunnel." But perhaps my language here is too "technical." Few analysands would think in such abstract terms. As one analysand explained it: "I think I'm coming to terms with my resentment toward my wife for the way she gets when she is critical. I know our goals are the same, and she works as hard as I do for them. I don't have to try to make-believe she isn't being critical when she is, but I also don't have to blind myself to my oversensitivity to her suggestions. I don't have to continue to picture her as an All-American ball-cutter and then not have sex with her to punish her. I know it's not my wife who's cutting me off from love when I do that; I do it to myself and it's damn foolish."

Another analysand said something much simpler: "I think I am almost at a point where I could go to any meeting or party now and be myself." This attractive young woman had struggled throughout her life with feelings of extreme shyness, embarrassment, and humiliation, alternating with occasional episodes of flamboyantly exhibiting her attractiveness and intelligence. The businesslike simplicity with which she verbalized the accomplishment that stemmed from lengthy, difficult work on her problems with self-display spoke volumes in itself.

When the analysand brings up the idea of ending, it is often a very delicate moment. The analysand is exposing to the analyst a personal evaluation of their joint efforts. There is a wish and need for an affirmation of the analysand's accomplishments and capacity to recognize them, as well as for a sound appraisal of the analytic work yet to be done. How does the analyst respond? A delicate moment in an analysis is unlike most other delicate moments. It differs from a learning situation in that the person is not best served by a didactic instruction (although straightforward information may be usefully included in the analyst's response). It is not the same as a delicate moment in a close personal relationship in that the person is not best served by an emotional reaction (although in a tempered way the analyst's feeling may be usefully included). The delicate moment of the analysand's considered expression of the possibility of ending requires the most delicate responses the analyst can provide—a careful analysis of its conceptual meaning and emotional significance. At first, however, it may seem that the analyst and the analysand are at odds. The analysand may want an "answer," but the analyst wants to sense the analysand's thoughts and feelings, to understand what the idea means to the analysand, before arriving at a response. The analyst is not avoiding a response. Rather, an honest response must grow out of the psychoanalytic process itself, with analysis of the meaning of the analysand's suggestion and the associations that derive from it.

HOW THE ENDING IS ARRANGED

To some degree making the termination arrangements is like renegotiating the analytic contract. First, there must be a mutual decision that the time is right for considering an ending. Then comes an agreement about the optimal date for that momentous event. As in making the initial arrangements, there's always the recognition that the assessments are based on the best possible human judgments and therefore to a degree uncertain. Thus, the decision can be reconsidered if that proves necessary.

What might the sequence be in all of this? Imagine that an

analysand comes in one day and mentions that there's something he's been thinking about for some time—that he thinks he's ready, at least in the foreseeable future, to end the analysis. The analyst recognizes the seriousness of the analysand's intent. Over a period of weeks, the two work together analytically to consider the analysand's feelings about his suggestion—his fears, his hopes, his fantasies. Although at times the analysand wavers, with ambivalent feelings, the suggestion remains alive. Expectations about the analyst's response are brought into awareness. The analysis touches on what it means to end something—the sense of adult accomplishment, as well as the feeling of loss. Certain conflict areas, in the process of being resolved, may come up, suggesting the need for further analytic work. Still, the idea of ending seems a possibility. Now the issue of the date as a concrete entity—a moment in time—must be faced.

Setting the Date

After completing a major readjustment in his life, Mr. North began to refer to ending analysis in a series of covert ways. I brought this to his attention, indicating that I was aware he might be fearful about terminating and so might be avoiding a direct reference to it. He agreed and entered into a fruitful consideration of the pros and cons and the various meanings ending had for him. The very clarification of his fears and hopes about terminating seemed a substantial accomplishment. Certainly the forthright way he expressed and recognized his feelings would have been impossible for him earlier in his analysis. Yet an omission soon stood out for me—in all his talk about whether he should end and why he should end and what it would be like when he ended, Mr. North never mentioned a specific date or time frame. Again, I suspected an underlying anxiousness and wondered if that might be the reason none of his associations included a "date." Ignoring my question about anxiousness, he responded in a slightly exasperated but largely resigned tone: "All right! How about three weeks from today?" The abruptness startled me. I inquired about his thinking on this. Annoyed and defensive, he answered that I was of course challenging him to act, to prove himself; he was only saying what he believed would satisfy me.

Mr. North's assumption about what I wanted led us back to a familiar problem, worked on earlier in the analysis, but with a new twist. He had long felt his manhood was on the line unless he adopted his older brother's macho value system and took a street-fighter's stance. His pattern was one of occasional impulsive, reckless acts after long periods of passivity and indecision. The new twist was his association of a "date" with a "dare." As long as we talked about terminating as a psychological concept, he felt sustained and valued for his mental abilities and his imagination, as he had been by a schoolteacher aunt. In other words, analyzing his fears about termination was equated with mental activity, but setting a date was keyed into physical action. The idea of a physical act precipitated a different kind of fear, triggering the association of an impulsive need to prove his manhood.

As he clarified these associations to the three-week ending date, Mr. North began to consider dates more suited to his real needs in completing the analysis. After reflecting on the remaining problems on which he wished to work, he stated hesitantly that he might possibly terminate in six months. Following a brief silence, he revised this, with more conviction. As he explained, he knew he might become defensive; also, he might be distracted by his job, which at times was unpreventably demanding. A year was probably a more practical target to shoot for—if less heroic. He wasn't afraid of having a little extra time for reflection; he didn't think he'd use it just to procrastinate and ruminate, as he might have done before. Now he felt he could treat the time as a chance to finish with dignity what he had worked so hard to achieve.

In my experience the usual termination phase varies considerably, depending both on the nature of the problems that arise during this delicate period of the analysis and on factors in the analysand's life situation. Thus, the date initially set is a tentative one and often is further reconsidered and amended. If, like Mr. North, the analysand contemplates ending in about a year, no official "date" is really being set—only a general goal to aim for. If the analyst agrees to this plan for ending, it is implied that at some later point the analyst and the analysand will further discuss the specific ending and set a formal date. Usually I try to make this implication explicit so the analysand knows that we have agreed both to a general time goal and to a reconsideration to set a formal date at a later time.

How this might work is illustrated by an analysand who initially timed her ending date to coincide with my summer vacation, then about fourteen months away. About six months before my vacation she became decidedly anxious. Her associations led to her increasing concern about meeting the ending date. Over the Christmas holiday, when she had not had any analytic sessions for ten days, she had been aware of missing me more poignantly than ever before. She knew she still had time to work on understanding these feelings, but she was certain the ending would be painful in any case. I suggested that the ending date she had picked—coinciding with my vacation—might accentuate the sense of being abandoned she often experienced at such times. She agreed and suggested that we reset the date for three months after my return from vacation. In reflecting on this, she mentioned it would then be Thanksgiving—a time when all her family got together. She added that by then she would have had the experience of being on her own during the vacation, and if she managed that okay, she'd have more confidence. Anyhow if we stopped in November she'd know that I was there—just in case she wanted to see me. It wasn't she hastened to reassure me (and herself) that she'd act on that wish except under very unexpected circumstances. It would just give her additional peace of mind to feel that she could.

CHANGES AT THE END

Revisiting Old Problems

With the two analysands I described, the ending phase took a year to a year and a half. Why so long? you may wonder. If the analysand correctly senses that he or she is ready to end, why should the date be set so far off? Is there something special that has to be done that requires so much time? The answer is "yes."

But the special task that lies ahead for the analysand is difficult to describe because it is unexpected. Rarely does an analysis proceed at a steady pace from the setting of the date to the ending. Rather, after the setting of the date—sometimes abruptly, sometimes more gradually—the analysand's regressive state of mind intensifies. Symptoms that had long ago disappeared may reappear. Old dream patterns, particularly anxious ones that have gone away after lengthy analytic effort to understand them, may reoccur. Conflicts the analysand thought had been worked through may be reactivated with all their original freshness—as if all the analytic work to resolve them had been erased. Sometimes an analysand will say, with considerable irony: "I thought I was ready to stop, but I'm as bad off as I was before I started." It's not hard to sympathize with the analysand's astonishment and consternation.

How can we explain this unexpected return of old problems? Why should an analysand who, for months, was tolerant and pragmatic in response to her teen-aged son, suddenly revert to her old pattern of reacting to ordinary requests as though they were provocations? Or why should an analysand who, during the middle phase of analysis, became a frequent dreamer, developing skills and pride in the analysis of his dreams, stop remembering his dreams as he had throughout most of the initial phase? One answer might be that conflicts are at best only partially worked through and that in the termination phase there is a last chance for them to come back to be further resolved. Yet, in saying this, there's the danger one will conjure up a little homunculus inside the mind who "knows" the remaining problems and, like a computer, sets them forward in sequence to be dealt with. It doesn't work that way. Another explanation, closer to the experience of the analysis, is that over the course of the therapeutic work the major problems, regardless of their original source, have come to be attached to the person of the analyst—that is, they were felt to exist in the ongoing analytic relationship. With the possibility of termination, the picture shifts. An old problem may have touched on the theme of loss, change, abandonment, independence or dependence, whatever—but then the separation was a fantasied one.

Now the problem must be reworked in the face of an actual impending separation. The idea is that familiar areas of difficulty receive renewed spark because of their associational link to the new "problem" of parting from the analyst.

A related explanation concerns the loss of analytic support for problem-solving. An analogy may help to convey my meaning. A young man takes up flight training. At first, he has a multitude of fears, as well as a great deal to learn. Gradually he becomes more and more adept at handling the plane, with assistance from the flight instructor as needed. He exposes himself to a wide range of flight conditions and masters the problems they entail. Then the instructor suggests a solo. Is it surprising that every concern and fantasy he has ever had about flying is reactivated, including an assortment of misgivings about himself and the instructor? He knows that for some time he has been increasingly responsible for flying the plane. He knows he has developed a number of skills—indeed, he is proud of them. But it is one thing to employ them when he knows the experienced instructor is right there; it is another thing to really be on his own. Contemplation of that creates a whole new situation. Or, more accurately it re-creates old fantasies or memories of fully testing what one has learned.

During the termination phase, then, the analysand must come to terms with two powerful subjective realities: first, that he or she can still fall prey to fears, symptoms, and attitudes that had seemed under better control; second; that although he or she has acquired new ways of responding to these stresses during analysis, they remain to be tested flying solo. How this happens may be seen in the analysis of Mrs. Randolph.

Mrs. Randolph had married shortly after high school. In her family the limited resources meant only the boys could go on to college. Even though scholarships were potentially available, Mrs. Randolph dutifully helped her mother and compliantly accepted her family's recommendation that she marry the son of a well-to-do family. She entered analysis in a rather serious state of depression, occasioned by the death of her father. During the early phase of her analysis it became apparent that her depressive tendencies preexisted her father's death and served as responses to strains in her marriage. Each partner felt equally coerced and resentful but nonetheless devoted to the other. As that facet of her problem was increasingly understood, another difficulty came to the fore. Her compliance with her parents' prohibition against further schooling hid a serious lack of confidence in her mental abilities. These doubts about her self-worth touched on every aspect of her being and, in their myriad conscious and unconscious forms, they become the main subject matter of her analysis. In the ending phase Mrs. Randolph described an incident that clearly illustrates her confrontation with the two powerful subjective realities: the return of symptomatic experiences and the use of new capacities to respond adaptively on one's own. Mrs. Randolph had returned to school with great hesitation. Although bright and capable, she suffered from a sense of not being as quick-witted as her husband. Nonetheless, she persevered and did well in a course allied to his area of expertise. In an analytic hour following her final examination, she described her sense of intense anxiety after a brief survey of the questions. A sinking sensation of hopelessness and failure had followed. For some minutes she had sat in a state of frozen depression. Then she had pictured herself telling me about it and my asking her what was triggering her apprehension. In her imagined conversations she found herself associating to the exam questions she had scanned. One was on a subject her husband had "lectured" on to her and she had resented his showing off. She pictured me suggesting that we knew she could now find other ways to respond to her resentment and envy without becoming an incapacitated martyr. With that interpretation, rendered to herself as though from me, she ceased to be depressed and began to work on her exam. During the actual analytic hour, Mrs. Randolph acknowledged to herself and to me that it was of great importance to her during her exam to feel that I was there with her—helping her, believing in her abilities, and rooting for her success. But it was *she* who had associated to the problem and *she* who had interpreted her resorting to a martyr posture in the face of her anger and envy. I asked her about the interpretation she had phrased for "me." She answered that, on reflection, it was more inspirational that

I ever sounded. Indeed she had done better for me than I did myself. Saying this, she giggled with mixed pride and embarrassment, and added that she didn't intend to be depressed over enjoying a tiny bit of one-upping me while being independent.

As do most analysts, I regard the capacity of an analysand, like Mrs. Randolph, to associate freely to be a significant criterion for a successful ending. Skill at introspective association develops gradually throughout the analysis; it waxes and wanes at all times. Even in the termination period, during episodes of resistance, the analysand may experience as much blockage to a productive associational flow as in the beginning. Usually such episodes of resistance yield relatively quickly to successful analysis, and they often provide valuable associations, following insight into their source. And as Mrs. Randolph illustrates, the analytic work within the sessions is accompanied by examples of self-analysis outside.

Gaining Flexibility in Using Analytic Tools

In the ending phase, other than during periods of resistance, there is generally a greater fluidity to the whole analytic process. Analysands often change their feelings toward the unconscious domain of their minds. Rather than deploring a balky aspect of themselves, constantly thwarting them with symptoms, they may come to regard their "unconscious" as a reliable source of information for the questions they seek to answer. Some analysands, for instance, comment that through their use of their unconscious they dreamt a dream in order to help themselves understand an issue they were working on. And their facility in associating to dreams and drawing inferences from their associations gives the analysis a sense of liveliness and the analysands a sense of efficacy and pleasure. The exchanges between analyst and analysand often take on an augmenting quality that contrasts with the tension of resistance. Not that the emotional intensity is diminished. In fact the very dynamics of ending ensure heightened affective exchanges. By now most of the major conflicts—whether around feelings of deprivation, failures in understanding, competitive strivings, or anger—

involve the analyst as the current representative of the past. Thus, the emotions the analysand experiences toward the analyst invest his or her associations with a moving sense of immediacy that grows rather than diminishes. Yet this intensity is counterbalanced by the flexibility the analysand now has to shift back and forth between an expression of attitudes about the analyst as a transference figure and the analyst as a professional (as analyst).

A month before the end of his analysis, Mr. Freeman described his resentment at his cousin for what he regarded as a patronizing remark. Mr. Freeman had worked hard during the analysis to free himself of his timidity about openly expressing resentment. Part of his old defensive technique had involved a rigid, monotonous way of speaking and narrowly focused ideation. Now, however, he spoke of his experience with his cousin with feeling in his voice. Then, he recalled that in the beginning of the analysis—five years before—he had felt I made a similarly patronizing remark. It had reminded him of his father and he had resented it. But, being unable to express his feeling, he had ignored it—and, he thought, forgotten it. Obviously he hadn't forgotten it. At this point he paused—then added wistfully: "I hate to think of myself as holding grudges." As he explained it: although he had been quiet about things that irritated him, he remembered them for years. Now, he believed, by responding actively to those kinds of annoyance, he wouldn't be so inclined to harbor old hates.

This example illustrates the flexibility of association that characterizes a successful analytic experience. Mr. Freeman was able to move from relating an emotion-laden current experience to an experience with the analyst that had meaning both on its own and as a representation of his childhood relationship with his father. He could reflect on his own cramped response and the problem (grudge-holding) that resulted. His final remark about the positive possibility of an assertive response contains an indication of his taking active responsibility for his future and by implication a reference to the analyst as a professional who facilitated the change.

You may be wondering what I mean by insisting on a fluid

associative capacity and the accessibility of emotional signals as indicators of analytic success. Certainly, for Mr. Freeman, these skills represented a welcome change—he had been rigid and blocked. But don't some people begin analysis with the ability to associate loosely and express anger and other emotions freely? In particular, what about someone who is flighty and hysterical? Isn't jumping about associatively a way of defensively avoiding an awareness of the deep sources of the person's problems? First of all, it should be clear that "free" association isn't simply loose association—the very idea of "jumping" suggests that something is being cut off and in that sense blocked. Nor does the accessibility of emotional signals mean that one simply gives full vent to one's feelings. An awareness of different emotional signals allows one the relative freedom to choose an appropriate emotional expression. Impulsively acting out one's rage is no more free than rigidly holding it in. In fact the freedom to consider one's circumstances thoughtfully usually is lost when emotions are vented indiscriminately. Another point is that, with successful analysis, analysands develop self-reflectiveness, through which they are able to take their spontaneous associations and double-back on them—as Mr. Freeman did in considering how he harbored grudges. Yet it is not the freer association, the greater accessibility of emotions, or the self-reflectiveness as such that makes for the more lasting change; it is the new integrations they facilitate.

Integrations occur in a number of areas. New discoveries about the meanings of events, past and present, are integrated with already-known meanings. Thoughts and feelings are integrated with each other and with their context, again both present and past. Perceptual capacities alter and expand—analysands become more adept at perceiving not only from their own perspective but also from the vantage point of others (a process that is facilitated by the double-perception of the analyst as transference figure and analyst). And analysands are able to expand the positioning of themselves as self-observers.

I believe that the most important integrations occur with respect to the analysand's sense of self. First of all, there is an integration of divergent aspects of oneself—the understanding that one can, at different times and under different circumstances, be friendly or guarded, kind or mean, serious or playful, wise or foolish, and still be the same person. Additional integrations occur across the axis of time. Here I am referring to the analysand's developing synthesis of a narrative, a connected story of his or her life. There is a weaving together of the threads from the self at different stages—the baby, the toddler, the preschool (oedipal) child, the school-age child, the teenager, and the adult—in relationships with other people, in a particular place at a particular time. It is not that the analysand can now write a literary autobiography or a medical-psychiatric case study. Rather, this integration across the arc of time brings an expanded sense of the meaning of each phase of one's life to each prior phase, to one's present, and by logical extrapolation to one's potential future. Both the long-remembered and the previously forgotten past, the good and the bad experiences, gain new and often different significances. At the same time, through an increased capacity for reflectiveness, the analysand can take a judicious distance from them.

DYNAMIC TENSIONS AT THE CLOSE

Two people have been together four or five hours per week, ten or eleven months per year, for four to seven years, or so. They have developed a unique intimacy. Now they are about to part, the depth of insight, the sharing of feelings and the discovery of hidden meanings they have achieved has been hard-won. Resistances and disparate viewpoints have had to be overcome; failures and successes have been reflected on. Each step has contributed to developing the sense of intimacy. From the beginning the plan has been to end, but as the time approaches there are inevitable tensions.

For each participant, the achievement of the end triggers a sense of accomplishment—even at moments triumph. But at the opposite end is the sense of loss and sadness triggered by the separation the achievement itself requires. For the analysand, ending means the loss of a unique experience of attentiveness, of being listened to and understood, of enjoying dignity, of finding meaning in his or her thoughts, feelings, and actions, however "odd." For the analyst, termination means the loss of a sense of closeness, of a sharing in the joy of another person's growth. In addition, each must now forgo the satisfaction of a curiosity that has been strongly activated. The analysand has been involved in an intense exploration of the sensibilities of a human being (him- or herself), with little opportunity to use the new tools of understanding to learn about the sensibilities of the partner in the task—the analyst. It is a strange situation. In exploring transferences the analysand associates to his or her subjective experience of the analyst, based on an ever-shifting mix derived partly from expectations from the past and partly from the present activity of the analyst as the analysand experiences it. The analysand would always like to know the other side. The analysand may think the analyst sees him or her as intelligent or aggressive or nice or whatever, but there is still the question: What does the analyst "really" think? And, although the analysand may think the analyst is intelligent or aggressive or nice or whatever, what is the analyst "really" like—especially outside the analytic situation? In all likelihood the analysand is destined not to know either. The analyst, on the other hand, has followed the most minute details of the developments in the analysand's life and learned about the analysand's plans. Now, as a result of the treatment, the analysand is in a position to move forward with those plans. But, just at the point where the analysand begins to do so, the contact ends. Perhaps it is something like coming to the end of a good novel, where there is all the promise of the future but no detail. It is possible that through letters or Christmas cards the analyst may hear about a former analysand's progress, but he or she can never know it in the form of analytic intimacy. Thus, an intrinsic aspect of the ending of analysis for both partners is a strong sense of emotional satisfaction and yet a wanting to know more.

There is still a further source of tension: How do analyst and analysand each feel about the result? This tension of course is not new. In a particular hour or period of the analysis, the analysand may want to accomplish one or another goal, whether exploratory (such as understanding a dream or an action) or nonexploratory (convincing the analyst of something or getting something from the analyst such as advice, comfort, or punishment). In the same hour or period, the analyst may also hope they will come to understand the reported dream or action. Or the analyst may see a quite different area covered in the associations. And the analyst will want to explore rather than accede to the analysand's effort to get advice, comfort, or punishment. During the termination period these pulls continue, but on a somewhat larger scale. In reexamining what they have achieved, each partner becomes more clearly aware of what they haven't accomplished. At times this exposes major dissatisfactions, but often it facilitates important analytic work in the ending phase.

Dr. Tyler, a research scientist, entered the termination phase eager to end. He appreciated the changes he had made and was looking forward to using the additional time and money he would have. Gradually, even though he continued to work analytically as before, his mood became more somber and irritable. A number of his associations pointed toward a theme of demeaning experts and authorities. He rejected the analyst's suggestion that he might be feeling negative about the analyst. Instead, he began to describe his work in depreciatory terms, despite what seemed to be steady progress in a slow-moving area of study. From the imagery in a series of dreams about sudden, dramatic changes, the analyst was able to assist Dr. Tyler in recognizing an important fantasy that he had maintained throughout the analysis—that the treatment would enable him to make a great discovery, a dramatic breakthrough. He was indeed disappointed that his valued self-discoveries had not translated into the fulfillments he yearned for in his research. Understanding this helped him to recognize more clearly than he had before how his secret dreams, with their high expectations, interfered with his ability to enjoy what he did achieve.

In another instance, the analyst had agreed to the termination but felt a sense of uneasiness, which she found difficult to define. All the criteria for ending seemed to be there. Why was she uneasy? One day the analyst was listening to the analysand, Mrs. Shawn, describe a trip with her daughter to a children's museum. Mrs. Shawn had had to scold her daughter; feeling somewhat guilty about this, she was glad when her daughter had become interested in an exhibit in another room and she had a minute to herself. Absentmindedly she had picked up a music box which played a lullaby. Then, for a moment during the session, she hummed the lullaby and talked about the memories of being held by her grandmother that it called forth. The analyst, listening in almost a reverie, suddenly had an insight into what had troubled her about Mrs. Shawn's ending. Whereas Mrs. Shawn had achieved considerable control over her anger and her sometimes crippling anxiety, and now functioned well in areas in which she previously had had great difficulty, her capacity to give and accept tenderness remained underdeveloped. Once she recognized this, the analyst was able to use Mrs. Shawn's awareness of the feelings she had about the lullaby and memories to open this area for very productive work before the ending day.

THE LAST HOURS

Analysands often wonder: "Will I get an evaluation before I end? Do I get to sit up and just talk to you? Do you tell me what you think about me or what I should do? What happens at the very end?" To not answer directly may seem frustrating, but analysts do not position themselves as "authorities" who answer and advise at the ending any more than at any other time. I do, however, welcome all these wonderings coming up in the associations. They provide sources for looking at analysands' fantasies about, for instance, an evaluation or "report card" (the one they hope to get from me and the one they fear to get). Equally valuable are analysands' ideas of the advice they hope I'll provide and the way we will part—shaking hands, saying goodbye mechanically without reference to the meaning of the occasion, kissing, crying, and so on. Because these wonderings are so important in opening up the last hours to a rich exploration of meanings—enhanced by the sense of immediate poignancy of the experience—I maintain the formal activities of the analysis until the last minute of the last hour.

Most commonly, the work of exposing and understanding disappointments that may come to the fore in the last months gives way in the last hours to a continuing integration and expansion of perspectives, alternating with a sense of loss. The sense of loss has been compared to mourning the death of a loved one. When physical contact is lost, the place the person occupies in the mourner's thoughts and feelings assumes an illuminating intensity. Memories of past exchanges—those that were sensitive and helpful, as well as those that were irksome and frustrating—all are tinged by nostalgia. Yet the mourner also draws strength from the experience with the valued but now lost, person, the strength to carry on alone, knowing that the memories are there to sustain. During the last hours an analysand may say "I know when I start to lose my temper and feel like I'm going to swat my son I'll hear your calm voice saying, 'Well, let's see, what got you so angry?'" Or; "Whenever I think of my mother now I don't see only the witch face that scared me out of my wits. I can still see it, but I'm not paralyzed by it anymore. I also see her when she was happy and when she was kind and when she taught me how to love books. Only I'm not sure if I'm seeing her, or a mixture of you and her. But it doesn't matter. I have it now and I didn't have it before."

Sometimes the association to loss is so intense that the analysand has to actively remind him- or herself that the analyst remains—only the analysis terminates. One analysand, in her dream images, kept consigning me to the grave. We discovered that the idea of my persisting was okay as long as she thought of running into me at a concert. But she could not bear to think of me in the office with another analysand—her successor. At this last moment the intense fears of losing her only-child status were revived once again.

Loss is not the only fantasy theme ending stirs up. There is also celebration. Many analysands plan a sumptuous meal or a glass of champagne—sometimes with a spouse or a special friend, sometimes alone. Yet usually these celebrations have a rather quiet character—perhaps a natural consequence of the bittersweet nature of the ending. Moreover, ending an analysis is a difficult experience to share. It lacks the communal elements of a wedding or a graduation or a national holiday. In fact it celebrates the completion of an experience that is so personal and unique that it is difficult to convey even to a friend who has gone through it its meaning at that particular moment for that particular (now "former") analysand.

LIGHTS AND SHADOWS AND AFTER-IMAGES

"How come," a friend who had completed her analysis a month ago asked me, "I still carry on conversations in my head with my analyst? Something happens and I say to myself, 'I'll tell him about that.' Or I wake up with a dream and I'll try to remember it for my hour. I have to remind myself: It's over; I won't be telling him. If I want to know what my dream is about I'll have to figure it out myself.'" She added: "Sometimes, if I think the dream harbors trouble, I *do* try to analyze it. But sometimes I say, 'To hell with it,' and get on with the day."

The analogy to mourning holds weight here: it takes about a year for the sense of acute loss to fade, for that hour of the day filled by the analysis for so long to become just another hour in the day, filled with its own content. For many former analysands the year passes relatively smoothly; for some it is rocky. For all there are moments of doubt and concern. Having learned to be attentive to indicators of turmoil in order to work on it, former analysands have to readjust their inner tuning. It is natural that some recontact their analyst during the year (or at any subsequent time). Some do this by letter, giving a report of progress or of concern. Others may request a consultation— sometimes because of a strong sense of need to resume the analysis or, commonly, for a reconsideration of a particular problem and reassurance about their continuing to try to apply the gains of analysis on their own.

Some of the experiences after the end of analysis indicate the persistence of old inclinations—giving rise to the aphorism that the unconscious never dies. One man, three weeks after termination, remembered an experience of a sexually exciting event on a trip with an adult member of his family. He recognized that this was exactly what his analyst had suggested had occurred, but he could never agree or recall it. His first urge was to call his analyst and tell him. Then he laughed—first with the recognition that he had "held out" on his analyst by keeping a "secret," but then with the recognition that he had provided himself an excuse to contact his analyst (an urge he did not act on). Another man, a month after ending, was asked by his secretary why he never scheduled business meetings at a particular time, although it would ease his schedule. It occurred to him that this had been the time of his anlytic hour; it was as if he were holding it sacred. A psychologist, who had ended her analysis some months before, was arguing with unusual vehemence for a particular theoretical position. A friend mentioned surprise both at her intensity and the stand she was taking, since she generally had taken the opposite position. With a slightly red face, the psychologist realized that the theory she was espousing was one she had read in a paper written by her former analyst.

These incidents are, I believe, more amusing than troublesome. The true test of the analytic result lies in the area of the person's central difficulties. When old problematic inclinations rearise—and many surely will—will the former analysand be able to react flexibly and selectively in new ways? Some of the beneficial effects of the analysis are silent, simply absorbed into the personality. Others require the mode of thinking used during the analysis—now in the form of self-analysis. Individuals vary in how actively they apply self-analysis to deal with stress and to check out the dynamic meaning of a dream or a slip or an attitude. Some do it with full awareness of "associating"; others are simply reflective. But, for most, it becomes second nature to accept that what one feels, thinks, does has meaning and that problems can be approached with a sense of the many determinants that pull one's motivation this way and that. It is a belief that one has a responsibility for one's own inner life—and a considerable degree of control over one's own destiny, despite the unpredictability of many external events—that I regard as the strongest after-image of analysis. Over time the details of the analytic resolutions of specific conflicts fade and the memories of victories of understanding in the long struggle to explore meanings become shadowy. What remains is the sense of control over one's perspective—keeping it as open and flexible as possible. That is the residue as the light on the images of the analyst and the analysis grows dim.

Afterthoughts

"I've read your book. You went through many of my initial questions about psychoanalysis, and you gave a glimpse of what an analysis is like by describing its three phases. In some ways it seemed like going behind the looking glass with Alice, only instead of mad-hatters and white rabbits, there were unconscious conflicts and transferences. You're probably right in saying that you could describe analysis as a process, but only by doing it will I get a true sense of the experience. I've gained some idea of what analysis is designed to do for me, but I still have questions about what it will do *to* me."

A PANDORA'S BOX OF FEARS

In its founding days and for many years after, a prevalent fear was that psychoanalysis would turn socially responsible people into sexual hedonists. Freud's findings destroyed the myth that children were sexual innocents. Moreover, Freud suggested that the root of neuroses lay in sexual conflict, that repressed (unconscious) sexual wishes lay behind the symptoms. The apprehension was that if, in psychoanalysis, people learned about their latent urges, they would abandon all the proper restraints a civilized society imposed on libertine behavior. From this perspective, an interest in psychoanalysis was considered prurient and treatment might lead to the destruction of moral values and licentiousness. These fears, of course, have proven groundless and are rarely voiced any longer. As one analysand stated, with some regret, getting to one's sexual fantasies in analysis turns out to be serious hard work. What analysis does is to enable analysands to take a balanced look at their desires, in relation to their general life goals and to their morals and ethics. In this way aspects of the analysand's sexual life, moral life, and goals that have been kept out of awareness or disconnected from each other become subject to introspective reasoning. At the same time the limitations of reasoning in controlling deep-seated urges are considered. Thus, logic, reason, and ethics gradually become partners rather than enemies in the pursuit of adult sensual and sexual fulfillment. Contrary to the popular misconception, psychoanalysis does not view sexuality as a detached entity; it is a pleasurable part of love and loving in relationships between people (present and past).

Even though analysis does not seduce the analysand into lascivious pursuits, according to another frequent fear, it encourages dependency. Looking at the length of analyses, there is an understandable apprehension that analysis may become a never-ending crutch. This fear is made all the more vivid by tales of well-known show business figures, with analysts in different cities, going for years and years. So families of analysands often wonder if analysis is addictive, especially when there is heightened distress during periods of the analyst's absence (weekends and vacations).

In one sense the perception of dependence on the analysand's part is accurate. Indeed, it is a common aspect of the investment the analysand makes—but, more important, it facilitates its own undoing in that it often becomes a central theme for the analysis. And there is another factor at play here. The analyst is aware from the first day to the last that the goal of the analysis is to end. It is intrinsic to the design. Freud's famous essay "Analysis Terminable and Interminable" is but one of many works written to alert and teach analysts to approach analysis with full awareness of problems that lead to stalemated or unduly protracted treatments.

A variant of the idea of the dependent analysand, who turns to the analyst to relieve every concern, is that analysis shifts the person's own responsibility for his or her difficulties toward blaming others—particularly the parents. In this view, rather than engaging in a sensitive exploration of prior relationships and events, the analyst is pictured as coddling the analysand's childishness and indulging his or her posture of perpetually lamenting victim. Recall, however, what I said about the shifting between childhood and adult perspectives. An analysand may well adopt a victim stance, but this very stance then becomes the focus of analysis. Indeed, the aim of analysis might be stated as a regaining of one's sense of responsibility. But this regaining may also entail a reexperiencing of the ways one tries to avoid it.

An interesting contrast to the fear one will be sucked into dependency through a warm, womblike atmosphere is the apprehension of being "abandoned" to a glacial ice-couch by an inhumanly silent analyst who never encourages or responds. The two-sided warm-cold image of the analyst is depicted in the story of two colleagues who meet at the end of the day on the elevator. One analyst asks: "How come at the end of every day you look so unruffled and I'm so frazzled? Listening to my analysands' troubles and their demands on me is so exhausting." After a pause for dramatic emphasis, the other analyst answers: "Well, who listens?" It is true the analyst does work by maintaining a posture of reflective listening not apt to be found in any ordinary experience in life. Yet the effect of the analyst's often silent presence is very hard to describe. I doubt that many analysands would agree to the caricature of the analysand as a rat in an experimental maze, forced to proceed without guidance while the analyst strokes his beard with either cruel indifference or sadistic pleasure. I've tried to hint at the delicate balance the analyst maintains between responding in a way that conveys empathy, yet centering his or her responses on a shared effort to explore and understand. What can't be described easily is the trust that underlies the analytic relationship. The analysand comes to know that the analyst is listening, and listening with respect, even if there is no immediate response.

Still another fear turns the unguided figure in the maze around, to the analysand being subtly swayed to an acceptance of the analyst's values and goals. Here the analyst becomes a Svengali, with a personal definition of normality; unless the analysand conforms to this definition, he or she is considered resistant and neurotic. A current, much-publicized version of this fear comes out in the contention that analysts invariably see the core of neuroses in woman as penis envy. Thus, it is argued, an analyst will insist that a woman give up all her ambitions other than those of wife, mother, and handmaiden to men. This fear is but one particularly cogent example of a complex problem that occurs in all analyses: analysts must use their theories and knowledge of society's values as guideposts without becoming witting or unwitting advocates for specific treatment outcomes. The changing picture of women, both in society and in psychological theory, is a salutary reminder of the need to anticipate that yesterday's uncertainties may become today's certainties only to become tomorrow's uncertainties.

Possibly the most commonly expressed fear is that analysis will make one hopelessly self-centered. After all, analysands spend hours each week talking about themselves and describing the world from their own perspectives. With all the concentration on "me," won't they become even more preoccupied with themselves and selfish in their dealings with others. Isn't analysis inevitably an "ego" trip? As before, it is instructive to look at a popular fear that is the antithesis: the apprehension embodied in the popular epithet for a psychoanalyst—the "shrink." Here the imagery is that of a deflating—whether of pretense or of ambition or even of one's good opinion of oneself. The grounding of this fear lies in the popular conception (or misconception) of "defenses"—the idea that behind high-sounding intentions often lurk unconscious shame-laden inclinations which analysands will discover about themselves. The fear is that areas of presumed superiority will be attacked and eroded, reducing the previous sources of pride to capacities that are simply ordinary. It is this anxiety that has led many creative people to believe analysis might dampen the flame of their inner sources of inspiration or reduce the meaning of their creative expressions to some infantile pursuit.

Let us stop here and reconsider our survey of apprehensions about what will happen to the analysand: the coddled dependent versus the rat in the maze versus the mesmerized subject of Svengali; the self-centered hedonist versus the fallible human, "shrunk" into "ordinariness." Clearly something is unwarranted in all these contradictions. And here we come to an implicit paradox. Each of the fears accurately represents something that may and often does happen in the course of a psychonalysis, as I have already to some extent indicated. But that is not a basis for condemning analysis, precisely because it overlooks what analysis can do *for* analysands. Again, we must look at how analysis works. The fears individuals have, especially the strong ones, are entwined with problematic inclinations—often unconscious. All these fears—even the contradictory ones—may seem to come "true" in any single analysis. (Contradictions of logic or reason hold no sway in the realm of the unconscious.) At some point in the analysis, for example, an individual may well feel the analyst is a "shrink" who has deflated his or her sense of goodness, or power, or whatever. But, remember, the analysand's expression of this belief facilitates analyzing what such an experience means. Then, at a different point, the same person may feel the analysis supplies a necessary sustenance, that he or she cannot live without it. Again, the expression of this belief facilitates analyzing what such an experience means. And so it goes on. The analyst may seem cold and unresponsive. Or the person may express concern about exciting sexual fantasies. Each view facilitates the search for understanding and meaning through an exploration of the accompanying associations and interplay of feelings toward the analyst and about the analysis.

So for the final paradox: each fear—or at least a good number of those I mentioned—must seem valid and pressing at many points in the analysis for all to prove unwarranted at its end. Put another way, it is necessary that one's apprehensions about sex, dependence, being left on one's own, being molded or in-fluenced, self-centered expansiveness or deflation, all receive experiential substantiation in order that none become the final outcome of the analysis.

WHY PSYCHOANALYSIS?

Looking back on nearly sixty years of involvement with psychoanalysis, Richard Sterba states: "My experience of many years as a psychoanalytic practitioner has increased my convic-tion that psychoanalysis, when used for the right cases, is superior to any other treatment method. Analysis is more than a symptomatic therapy. Analysis with a good therapist leads to self-insight, which enhances the growth of the personality, widens the patient's world view and understanding of others, and increases true creativity. It cannot be replaced by any of the many short-cut therapies that are temporarily in vogue and fol-low each other in rapid succession."[1]

As Sterba implies, I believe that comparing other therapies to a successful psychoanalysis is like comparing a chapter to a com-pletely integrated book or a movement to a symphony. The whole of the analytic experience is greater than the sum of its parts. Returning to my initial analogy of a journey, the analytic excursion is unique in attempting, through introspection, the most exhaustive voyage of discovery of the self. Analysis af-fords its analysands the opportunity to ask all the questions about themselves that self-reflection—given the time—can crys-tallize. In this way the chapters of the life story, the stages of the journey, can be pieced together into a more coherent whole. Through this experience of self-insight in depth, this carrying out in modern-day form of the ancient injunction "Know Thy-self!," analysands who have had a successful analytic experience

---

[1]Richard Sterba, *Reminiscences of a Viennese Psychoanalyst* (De-troit: Wayne State University Press, 1982), pp. 134–35.

can face not only moral truths of their lives but can more effectively integrate all the fragments of their urges and goals.

As we learn from the reflective introspection of each analysand, we analysts have an opportunity to add to the knowledge of the general psychology of man. This touches on the ever-changing aspect of our theories—or "metapsychology" as Freud called it—and is of course beyond the compass of this descriptive guide. The journey here started with a person thinking about psychoanalysis for him or herself. It finished with a description of the completion of the analytic experience. The experience then opens the path to new beginnings of living one's life strengthened against succumbing to its inevitable vicissitudes through knowledge and integration of the self.

Appendix
Psychoanalytic Organizations
and Training

The following brief descriptions of selected psychoanalytic organizations and training programs are designed to help you in your search for a qualified psychoanalyst.

AMERICAN PSYCHOANALYTIC ASSOCIATION
1 East 57th Street
New York, NY 10022
(212) 752-0450

Founded in 1911, the American Psychoanalytic Association has a membership of about 3,000 analysts, with accredited training institutes and affiliate psychoanalytic societies throughout the U.S. (see listings below). Its institutes must meet rigorous standards to be approved, and the educational program at each institute is periodically reviewed to ensure the highest quality. To become a full, certified member of the Association, an analyst must have graduated from an approved institute and have passed a comprehensive evaluation by the Association.

In addition to setting and maintaining high profesional standards, the Association promotes a variety of educational activities and endeavors to keep its members informed of new ideas and developments in psychoanalytic practice, theory, and research. It holds two annual national meetings, where papers on psychoanalytic topics are presented and discussed. It publishes the *Journal of the American Psychoanalytic Association*. From its beginning, the American Psychoanalytic Association has been affiliated with the International Psycho-Analytical Association, which is the official representative of worldwide psychoanalysis.

As noted earlier, to find a qualified psychoanalyst, you may wish to consult the Roster of the American Psychoanalytic Association, which lists its members with addresses and telephone numbers. The Roster is available at most medical school libraries, as well as through the Association or its accredited instititutes. Either the Association or one of its institutes will, upon request, supply you with names of members in your area.

For those who cannot afford the usual private fees, treatment at a lower cost may be available through one of the Association's training institutes. Inquiries should be made either to the American Psychoanalytic Association or to the accredited institute in your area.

Training Program

Freud offered a three-part definition of psychoanalysis as (1) a way of investigation mental processes, especially unconscious ones; (2) a treatment method based on this exploration; and (3) a set of observations gathered through this process, giving rise to a body of psychological theory. The educational standards set by the American Psychoanalytic Association encompass all three aspects of this definition. In addition to completing course work in psychoanalytic theory and technique, analysts-in-training must undergo a meaningful personal analysis and conduct psychoanalyses with at least three patients under the close supervision of experienced psychoanalysts.

To be accepted for training at an accredited psychoanalytic institute, candidates must meet high professional and personal standards, including evidence of integrity and maturity. In general, they must have received an M.D. degree from a medical school approved by the American Medical Association and must complete a four-year residency program in psychiatry before they finish their psychoanalytic training. There are also a small number of nonmedical candidates, with outstanding qualifications in other fields, who have received special approval from the Association. All candidates, whatever their background, undertake an additional six to ten years of psychoanalytic training.

The *curriculum* of the Association's institutes integrates courses on theory, clinical applications, and psychoanalytic technique. Students gain a thorough understanding of the fundamentals of psychoanalysis as developed by Sigmund Freud and his co-workers. Advanced instruction is provided through case seminars and clinical conferences. The *personal analysis*, required for each candidate, is conducted with an approved training analyst and includes at least 300 hours of analysis, usually considerably more. The goal is to achieve a high degree of character stability and maturity, as well as to free the candidate from any emotionally conditioned patterns that might interfere with psychoanalytic work. As indicated, each candidate also engages in *supervised clinical work* with a suitable variety of patients, under the guidance of at least two different supervising analysts. The aim is to instruct candidates in the psychoanalytic method, as well as to foster their therapeutic skills, determine the effectiveness of their course work and personal analysis, and assess their maturity and stability over time. All these phases of the training program must be deemed successfully completed before a candidate will be graduated from an institute (lists of accredited training institutes and affiliated societies follow on p. 146).

AMERICAN ACADEMY OF PSYCHOANALYSIS
30 East 40th Street, Suite 608
New York, NY 10016
(212) 670-4105

The American Academy of Psychoanalysis is a membership organization of individual psychoanalysts; it does not have affiliated institutes or societies. Applications for membership are accepted from physician graduates from the American Psychoanalytic Association's institutes (see above), as well as from the Department of Psychoanalytic Training of New York Medical College, the William Alanson White Institute (see below), the American Institute for Psychoanalysis of the Karen Horney Psychoanalytic Institute and Center, the Detroit

Psychoanalytic Society and Institute, the Tulane Program in Psychoanalytic Medicine, and the Postgraduate Center for Mental Health (see below). The training standards for these institutes are set by the institutes rather than the Academy, although the Academy's Committee on Education may make suggestions, which any institute may decide to incorporate into its training program.

NEW YORK FREUDIAN SOCIETY
200 East End Avenue
New York, NY 10028
(212) 348-1230

Established in 1959, the New York Freudian Society is an independent psychoanalytic society and institute, chartered by the Board of Regents of the New York State Department of Education. Members of the Society include approved graduates of its Training Institute, as well as qualified analysts who have completed training in comparable programs and been accepted by the Society. Committed to the teachings of Sigmund Freud, the Training Institute offers psychoanalytic training to qualified candidates from various mental health disciplines and related academic fields. The Society itself endeavors to further its members' psychoanalytic understanding through monthly scientific programs, as well as an annual conference on a theme of broad interest. It also attempts to disseminate psychoanalytic findings and encourages psychoanalytic research.

In conjunction with its training program, the New York Freudian Society maintains a psychoanalytic consultation service, which offers low-cost treatment to the community by supervised candidates. Inquiries about this service should be addressed to the Chairperson of the Consultation Service. Application for treatment may also be made by calling (212) 348-1260.

Training Program

According to its Bulletin, "it is the Institute's conviction that Freud's theory of the mind and clinical technique occupy a position of central pertinence and cogency; and that they remain distinguishable as an orderly, self-consistent body of knowledge, with their own methods for clarification, amplification and development." Under this conviction, the Institute offers psychoanalytic training to psychiatrists, psychologists, and clinical social workers who meet its admission standards. Although the Institute welcomes participation by carefully selected applicants from a broad range of humanistic disciplines, to receive a certificate of completed training to practice any form of psychotherapy, the candidate must be licensed or certified under one of the mental health professions (in addition to successfully completing the Institute's training requirements).

In general, candidates must be at least twenty-five years old, hold a Master's degree or higher in an approved discipline from an accepted institution, and meet standards of personal suitability. A *personal analysis* of at least 400 hours, with an approved training analyst, is required. The *curriculum* covers psychoanalytic theory, clinical applications, and technique, with case seminars to provide advanced instruction. At the *control analysis* level, a candidate must treat two separate analytic cases (for a minimum of one and two years respectively) under the supervision, or "control," of two different analysts approved by the Institute. (One case must be a low-fee patient referred by the consultation service.) The final step is the *case presentation evaluation*, designed to assess candidates' grasp of theory in its clinical application and their general competence in using analytic concepts and techniques.

NEW YORK UNIVERSITY POSTDOCTORAL PROGRAM IN PSYCHOTHERAPY AND PSYCHOANALYSIS

Graduate School of Arts and Science
Department of Psychology
10 Washington Place, 2nd Floor
New York, NY 10003
(212) 598-2645

Under the auspices of New York University, the Postdoctoral Program in Psychotherapy and Psychoanalysis is intended to provide the broad approach to psychoanalysis possible within a university setting. Designed specifically to train qualified psychologists in the theory and practice of psychoanalysis and psychotherapy, the program stresses acquisition and understanding of therapeutic skills, as well as knowledge of theory and research.

In conjunction with the program, the Postdoctoral Clinic provides individual psychoanalytic psychotherapy with candidates under supervision for a limited number of individuals at reduced fees. Inquiries about the clinic should be made at the above address.

Training Program

As stated in the informational brochure, "The curriculum is designed to encourage an intellectual community in which theoretical diversity may thrive and where greater clarity of conceptualization in current psychoanalytic thinking is achieved." In line with this, "the faculty members represent a variety of theoretical orientations."

The program is open to applicants with a doctoral degree in clinical psychology or a related area of psychology. They must have two years of supervised individual psychotherapy experience and qualify for certification as psychologists in New York State.

To receive a Certificate in Specialization in Psychotherapy and Psychoanalysis, students must successfully complete the required course work, personal analysis, and supervision. Within the *curriculum*, students may select either a Freudian or Interpersonal-Humanistic orientation, or they may combine courses from both orientations, along with "nonaligned" courses. They must also undergo an intensive *personal analysis*, of at least 260 hours, with an approved analyst. At the *supervision* level, program participants are expected to work with three patients in intensive psychotherapy under three different supervisors. (One or two of these patients are referred through the low-cost clinic.)

POSTGRADUATE CENTER FOR MENTAL HEALTH
124 East 28th Street
New York, NY 10016
(212) 689-7700

Founded in 1948, the Fellowship Training Program of the Post-graduate Center for Mental Health offers a comprehensive, diversified approach to psychoanalytic and psychotherapeutic education. According to the Center's Bulletin, the goal is "to develop skilled therapists whose work integrates sound and flexible principles of clinical technique within a conceptual framework informed by a thorough grounding in the insights of psychoanalytic theory." The atmosphere is a multidisciplinary one, with both faculty and candidates from the fields of social work, psychology, and psychiatry.

In addition to psychoanalytic training, the Center provides training in child and adolescent analytic therapy, group and family therapy, and organizational consultation to its candidates, as well as instruction in the teaching and supervision of the therapeutic process to its graduates. Graduates of the Center's programs are eligible to join its Professional Association and the Postgraduate Psychoanalytic Society, a member of the International Federation of Psychoanalytic Societies.

Training Program

The training program coordinates formal course work, varied clinical experience, a personal analysis, and individual and group supervision. Although reflecting diverse points of view, the faculty "remains committed to the conviction that a comprehensive understanding of the origins and evolution of Freudian ideas is an important part of a serious psychoanalytic education," according to the Center's Bulletin.

To enter the training program, all applicants must evidence emotional, intellectual, and moral suitability and have had appropriate prior clinical experience. Specific degree and experience requirements, including appropriate New York State licensing and certification, must be met by applicants from each of the three areas—psychiatry (M.D.), psychology (Ph.D. or Psy.D. in psychology), and psychiatric social work (Master's in social work).

In addition to providing a thorough grounding in Freudian concepts, the four-year program of *class work* emphasizes contemporary developments in ego psychology, object relations, and self psychology. Independent study of other approaches is encouraged. An integral part of the program is the *personal training analysis* (at least 500 hours with an approved analyst), with the aim of resolving any emotional impediments to effective clinical work and increasing understanding of the psychoanalytic process through first-hand experience. Candidates are expected to augment their *clinical experience* by treating a variety of patients, including at least ten hours per week of work with clinic patients. *Supervision,* both individually and in groups, with different approved analysts, extends throughout the course of training, with a minimum of 300 hours of supervision required. Finally, for certification in the program, all candidates must give a *case presentation*, which is reviewed and evaluated with the candidate by a faculty panel.

WILLIAM ALANSON WHITE INSTITUTE OF PSYCHIATRY, PSYCHOANALYSIS, AND PSYCHOLOGY
20 West 74th Street
New York, NY 10023
(212) 873-0725

The William Alanson White Institute, founded in 1943, is an association of psychoanalysts and other behavioral scientists. In the words of its brochure, its training program is "based on the conviction that the study of lives in depth provides the best foundation for all forms of psychotherapy and for research into difficulties in living."

Beyond its psychoanalytic training program, the Institute offers continuing professional education for psychoanalysts, psychiatrists, psychologists, social workers, psychiatric nurses, and other mental health professionals, with courses in recent developments in psychoanalytic understanding. It also sponsors various research projects. The international quarterly *Contemporary Psychoanalysis* is the journal of the Institute and the William Alanson White Psychoanalytic Society. The Institute also publishes a triquarterly Newsletter on its activities.

Through its clinical therapeutic services, the Institute provides low-cost therapy to the community, including specific services for various age groups (from children through adults over sixty), industrial labor unions, and Hispanic-Americans. Inquiries should be addressed to the Director, Clinical Services, William Alanson White Institute.

Training Program

The Institute's philosophical approach encompasses the major contributions of Sigmund Freud, as well as pre- and post-Freudian contributions to the study of personality. A particular emphasis, drawing on the work of two of the Institute's founders, Harry Stack Sullivan and Erich Fromm, is the study of people as social beings and of human behavior as social communication.

The certificate program is open to psychiatrists and psychologists. Psychiatrists must hold an M.D. degree from a medical school accredited by the American Medical Association and have one year of psychiatric residency in an approved hospital, with three years to be completed before graduation from the Institute. Psychologists must have a Ph.D. in clinical psychology from an approved university and have completed a one-year internship in an approved psychiatric hospital, as well as two years of supervised work in clinic (an additional year must be completed before graduation).

The required *curriculum* serves as a staged progression of courses in psychoanalytic theory, clinical applications, and technique, with advanced electives including case seminars. Each candidate must undergo a *personal analysis* with an approved training analyst, with the goal of resolving any personality factors that might interfere with psychoanalytic work. Under the *supervision* requirement, a candidate must conduct psychoanalysis with four patients under the direction of at least three different supervising analysts for at least 200 hours. (The first case is referred by the Institute's clinical services.) In addition, candidates are expected to perform at least 120 hours of psycho-therapy in the clinical services. Candidates who satisfactorily complete this four- to six-year program are granted a Certificate in Psychoanalysis.

ACCREDITED TRAINING INSTITUTES OF THE AMERICAN PSYCHOANALYTIC ASSOCIATION 1982–1984

Baltimore-District of Columbia Institute for Psychoanalysis
Address: 821 N. Charles St., Baltimore, MD 21201
Telephone: (301) 727-1740

The Boston Psychoanalytic Society and Institute, Inc.
Address: 15 Commonwealth Ave., Boston, MA 02116
Telephone: (617) 266-0953

The Chicago Institute for Psychoanalysis
Address: 180 N. Michigan Ave., Chicago, IL 60601
Telephone: (312) 726-6300

Cincinnati Psychoanalytic Institute
Address: 3001 Highland Ave., Cincinnati, OH 45219
Telephone: (513) 961-8886

The Cleveland Psychoanalytic Institute
Address: 11328 Euclid Ave., Cleveland, OH 44106
Telephone: (216) 229-5959

Columbia University Center for Psychoanalytic Training and Re-
  search
Address: 722 W. 168th St., New York, NY 10032
Telephone: (212) 927-5000

The Denver Institute for Psychoanalysis University of Colorado
  School of Medicine

Address: University of Colorado School of Medicine
4200 E. Ninth Ave., Denver, CO 80262
Telephone: (303) 394-7776, 7777, 7778

The Houston-Galveston Psychoanalytic Institute
Address: 5300 San Jacinto, Suite 145, Houston, TX 77004
Telephone: (713) 524-0790

The Institute of the Philadelphia Association for Psychoanalysis
Address: 15 St. Asaphs Rd., P.O. Box 36, Bala Cynwyd, PA 19004
Telephone: (215) 839-3966, 667-8708

Los Angeles Psychoanalytic Society and Institute
Address: 2014 Sawtelle Blvd., Los Angeles, CA 90025
Telephone: (213) 478-6541

The Michigan Psychoanalytic Institute
Address: 16310 W. 12 Mile Rd., No. 204, Southfield, MI 48076
Telephone: (313) 559-5855

New Orleans Psychoanalytic Institute, Inc.
Address: 3624 Coliseum St., New Orleans, LA 70115
Telephone: (504) 899-5815

The New York Psychoanalytic Institute
Address: 247 East 82nd St., New York, NY 10028
Telephone: (212) 879-6900

Philadelphia Psychoanalytic Institute
Address: 111 N. 49th St., Philadelphia, PA 19139
Telephone: (215) 474-5748

Pittsburgh Psychoanalytic Institute
Address: Suite 200, 211 N. Whitfield St., Pittsburgh, PA 15206
Telephone: (412) 661-4224

Psychoanalytic Institute of New England, East, Inc.
Address: P.O. Box 56, Arlington Heights, MA 02175
Telephone: (617) 646-6150

The Psychoanalytic Institute
New York University Medical Center

Address: Bellevue Psychiatric Hospital
        30th St. & First Ave., New York, NY 10016
Telephone: (212) 340-6243

St. Louis Psychoanalytic Institute
Address: 4524 Forest Park Ave., St. Louis, MO 63108
Telephone: (314) 361-7075

San Diego Psychoanalytic Institute
Address: 817 Silverado St., La Jolia, CA 92037
Telephone: (714) 459-7676

San Francisco Psychoanalytic Institute
Address: 2420 Sutter St., San Francisco, CA 94115
Telephone: (415) 563-5815

Seattle Psychoanalytic Institute
Address: 4029 E. Madison St., Seattle, WA 98112
Telephone: (206) 324-6611

Southern California Psychoanalytic Institute
Address: 9024 Olympic Blvd., Beverly Hills, CA 90211
Telephone: (213) 276-2455

Topeka Institute for Psychoanalysis
Address: Box 829, Topeka, KS 66601
Telephone: (913) 273-7500

University of North Carolina-Duke University
Psychoanalytic Training Program
Address: Department of Psychiatry, UNC School of Medicine
        239 Old Nurses Dorm, Chapel Hill, NC 27514
Telephone: (919) 966-3379

Washington Psychoanalytic Institute
Address: 4925 MacArthur Blvd., N.W., Washington, DC 20007
Telephone: (202) 338-5453

The Western New England Institute for Psychoanalysis
Address: 340 Whitney Ave., New Haven, CT 06511
Telephone: (203) 562-2103

AFFILIATE SOCIETIES OF
THE AMERICAN PSYCHOANALYTIC ASSOCIATION

The Association for Psychoanalytic Medicine (New York)
Address: 525 West End Ave., New York, NY 10024
Telephone: (212) 799-3700

Atlanta Psychoanalytic Society
Address: 1493 LaVista Rd., N.E., Atlanta, GA 30324
Telephone: (404) 329-5886

Baltimore-District of Columbia Society for Psychoanalysis
Address: 821 N. Charles Street, Baltimore, MD 21201
Telephone: (301) 727-1740

The Boston Psychoanalytic Society and Institute, Inc.
Address: 15 Commonwealth Ave., Boston, MA 02116
Telephone: (617) 266-0953

The Chicago Psychoanalytic Society
Address: 180 N. Michigan Ave., 23rd floor, Chicago, IL 60601
Telephone: (312) 726-6300

Cincinnati Psychoanalytic Society
Address: 3001 Highland Ave., Cincinnati, OH 45219
Telephone: (513) 961-8861

Cleveland Psychoanalytic Society
Address: 11328 Euclid Ave., Cleveland, OH 44106
Telephone: (216) 229-2111

Dallas Psychoanalytic Society
Address: 8226 Douglas Ave., Dallas, TX 75225
Telephone: (214) 691-8606

The Denver Psychoanalytic Society
Address: 4900 Cherry Creek South Dr., Denver, CO 80222
Telephone: (303) 320-4119

Florida Psychoanalytic Society
Address: 1900 Coral Way, Miami, FL 33145
Telephone: (305) 856-2986

The Houston-Galveston Psychoanalytic Society
Address: Houston Child Guidance Center
        3214 Austin Street, Houston, TX 77004
Telephone: (713) 529-6920

The Long Island Psychoanalytic Society
Address: 191 Briarwood Crossing, Lawrence, NY 11559
Telephone: (516) 374-2848

Los Angeles Psychoanalytic Society and Institute
Address: 2014 Sawtelle Blvd., Los Angeles, CA 90025
Telephone: (213) 478-6541

Michigan Association for Psychoanalysis, Inc.
Address: P.O. Box 611, Southfield, MI 48037

Michigan Psychoanalytic Society
Address: 16310 W. 12 Mile Rd.—No. 204, Southfield, MI 48076
Telephone: (313) 559-5855

The New Jersey Psychoanalytic Society
Address: Two Princess Rd., Lawrenceville, NJ 08648
Telephone: (609) 896-1717

New Orleans Psychoanalytic Society
Address: 3624 Coliseum St., New Orleans, LA 70115
Telephone: (504) 899-5815

New York Psychoanalytic Society
Address: 247 East 82nd St., New York, NY 10028
Telephone: (212) 879-6900

North Carolina Psychoanalytic Society
Address: Suite 103, Central Medical Park, 2609 North Duke St.,
   Durham, NC 27704
Telephone: (919) 471-3487

Philadelphia Association for Psychoanalysis
Address: 15 St. Asaphs Rd., P.O. Box 36, Bala Cynwyd, PA 19004
Telephone: (215) 839-3966, (215) 667-8708

Philadelphia Psychoanalytic Society, Inc.
Address: 111 North 49th St., Philadelphia, PA 19139
Telephone: (215) 474-5748

Pittsburgh Psychoanalytic Society
Address: Suite 220, 211 N. Whitfield St., Pittsburgh, PA 15206
Telephone: (412) 661-2300

The Psychoanalytic Association of New York, Inc.
Address: 708 E. 19th St., Brooklyn, NY 11230
Telephone: (212) 434-0464

St. Louis Psychoanalytic Society
Address: 4524 Forest Park Ave., St. Louis, MO 63108
Telephone: (314) 361-7075

San Diego Psychoanalytic Society
Address: 817 Silverado St., La Jolla, CA 92037
Telephone: (714) 459-7676

San Francisco Psychoanalytic Society
Address: 2420 Sutter St., San Francisco, CA 94115
Telephone: (415) 563-5815

Seattle Psychoanalytic Society
Address: 4033 East Madison St., Seattle, WA 98112
Telephone: (206) 323-1706

Southern California Psychoanalytic Society
Address: 9024 Olympic Blvd., Beverly Hills, CA 90211
Telephone: (213) 276-2455

The Topeka Psychoanalytic Society
Address: 5800 S.W. Sixth Ave., P.O. Box 829, Topeka, KS 66601
Telephone: (913) 273-7500

The Virginia Psychoanalytic Society
Address: 106 N. Thompson St., Richmond, VA 23221
Telephone: (804) 358-2161

Washington Psychoanalytic Society
Address: 4925 MacArthur Boulevard, N.W.,
          Washington, D.C. 20007
Telephone: (202) 338-5453

The Westchester Psychoanalytic Society
Address: 45 Popham Rd., Scarsdale, NY 10583
Telephone: (914) 472-2323

Western New England Psychoanalytic Society
Address: 340 Whitney Ave., New Haven, CT 06511
Telephone: (203) 562-2103

The Western New York Psychoanalytic Society
Address: 300 Crittenden Blvd., Rochester, NY 14642
Telephone: (716) 275-5888

STUDY GROUPS OF THE AMERICAN PSYCHOANALYTIC ASSOCIATION

Oregon Psychoanalytic Study Group
Address: 1125 S.W. Saint Clair Ave., Portland, OR 97205
Telephone: (503) 227-7066

Society of Psychoanalysts of Puerto Rico
Address: Box 11481, Caparra Heights Station, San Juan, PR 00922
Telephone: (809) 781-3555

Wisconsin Psychoanalytic Study Group
Address: 2277 North Lake Dr., Milwaukee, WI 53202
Telephone: (414) 271-9711